Training
without Trauma

BY LISA S. NEWMAN, N.D., Ph.D.

Foreword by Deborah C. Mallu, D.V.M., C.V.A.

THE CROSSING PRESS
FREEDOM, CALIFORNIA

For information on bulk purchases or group discounts for this and other Crossing Press titles, please contact our Special Sales Manager at 800/777-1048.

Visit our website on the Internet: **www.crossingpress.com**

Cautionary Note: The nutritional information, recipes, and instructions contained within this book are in no way intended as a substitute for medical counseling. Please do not attempt self-treatment of a medical problem without consulting a qualified health practitioner.

The author and The Crossing Press expressly disclaim any and all liability for any claims, damages, losses, judgments, expenses, costs, and liabilities of any kind or injuries resulting from any products offered in this book by participating companies and their employees or agents. Nor does the inclusion of any resource group or company listed within this book constitute an endorsement or guarantee of quality by the author or The Crossing Press.

ISBN 1-58091-007-6

Library of Congress Cataloging-in-Publication Data
Newman, Lisa S.
    Training without trauma / by Lisa S. Newman.
       p. cm. -- (The Crossing Press pocket series)
    At head of title: Natural pet care.
    ISBN 1-58091-007-6 (pbk.)
    1. Dogs--Training. 2. Cats--Training. 3. Dogs--Behavior.
  4. Cats--Behavior. I. Title. II. Title: Natural pet care. III. Series.
SF431.N47   1999
  636.7'0887--dc21   99-37374
                                         CIP

Contents

Foreword

It is with great pleasure that I introduce Lisa Newman's remarkable series. She has dedicated her life to helping you care for your animal companions—we can all benefit from her years of experience.

We are living in a time of great change, especially in the realm of health care. As a practicing veterinarian for more than two decades, I have witnessed both myself and my clients begin to seek less invasive, more natural methods for healing our dogs and cats. Once we understood that all beings are interconnected on this planet, we became aware that our thoughts, emotions, and family dynamics played an important role in the health of our animal companions. We began to realize the importance of forming a team first with the members of our animal family, aided by other healing professionals including natural health counselors and animal communicators.

Over the years I have heard people say, "I didn't know you could use that natural remedy or treatment on animals." Feel confident that you can help your animal companions where the healing is best—in your loving home. Our animals nurture us by giving us unconditional love. In turn, we can nurture them with fresh, live food and supplements, so that they can live a long and healthy life. Lisa Newman will show you the way so that you can be empowered as a healer.

Deborah C. Mallu, D.V.M., C.V.A.

Understanding Dogs and Cats

Traditional animal training employs physical punishments and rewards to make certain behaviors occur. Frequently with this type of training, the handler makes a pet scared or confused. This does not have to occur if a different kind of training is used, training in which there is gentle treatment and appropriate communication between the trainer and the pet. Traditional training methods can interfere with the pet's ability to focus, learn, understand, and, most important, to retain what it is being taught. As a result, the animal performs poorly and receives further physical punishment or brief abandonment, which only reinforces the pet's fear and inadequacies.

Behavioral problems in pets often are considered only from the owner's point of view. Frustrated owners react as if their pets are being spiteful. When they have to clean up messes and suffer embarrassment, they retaliate in some way rather than guiding the pet toward proper behavior. Once you understand why your pet behaves the way she does you can guide her toward more appropriate behavior and your relationship will become easier and mutually beneficial.

The purpose of this book is to help humans better understand their pets. With so many training manuals available, including an excellent pamphlet that is free from any local Humane Society, it didn't seem necessary for me to write another "how to put the pet through the paces" book. I will focus instead on the seven emotional filters through which a pet understands its experiences, and the eight emotional dynamics that are prevalent in pets with specific behavioral problems.

Once you understand how your pet comprehends what you want, and you improve your ability to communicate, most of the behavioral problems will begin to resolve. Even if you two have struggled with these issues for years, it is possible to learn a new language that will help change old behavior patterns.

COMMUNICATING WITH YOUR PET

Communication is more than visualizing what your pet may be thinking or feeling. It includes understanding each other's body language and developing a common spoken and visual language together.

You have seen a cat arch its spine and raise its fur when confronted by a dog. Usually the dog retreats. Both animals understand what each other's signals mean. If the cat purred instead, no matter how much the cat wants the dog to back off, the dog would continue to annoy the cat. When you use proper signals, your animal will understand what you mean. By paying attention to signals received from your pet, you will be able to gauge how well they learn what you are telling them. Then you both have an environment more conducive to training (and learning) without trauma.

Several other issues are also involved in reversing, even preventing, behavioral problems. Traits that are specific to certain breeds, life cycles, illness, environmental chemicals, dietary ingredients, or medications may cause behavioral problems. Many safe remedies are available to help alter a pet's perception and reactions to their environment. Eliminating unnecessary anxiety, fear, or anger from your pet's perception of their environment will help encourage the proper responses.

Once you understand each other better and use these training tools to encourage proper behavior, a stronger foundation of mutual trust is built, which increases the animal's desire to behave appropriately in order to please you.

UNDERSTANDING YOUR PET

Today's dog and cat breeds are the result of the intense domestication and increasing genetic manipulation, resulting in many dogs and cats struggling with physical and/or behavioral problems. Specialization has changed the genetic codes in favor of appearance, size, and color and also mutated the genetic information for health and emotional stability. As a result, many pet owners today are faced with behavioral problems.

In-breeding and excessive genetic manipulation has minimized our animals' natural ability to heal themselves of disease and maintain emotional stability. Moreover, years of vaccinations or reactions to vaccines often precede the development of aggressive or fearful behaviors. Chemical baths, flea/tick potions, dips or sprays, medications, and most importantly, poor-quality ingredients, artificial colors, preservatives, and by-products found in most pet foods and treats can cause emotional and behavioral problems.

The nervous system can be severely altered or damaged by genetics as well as by chemicals to which your pet is exposed. Emotional issues can result from physical illness, trauma, or pain. Behavioral problems are on the rise, as more pets are aggressive or fearful. They have trouble learning to get along with their human families, owners, and veterinarians. Drugs such as *Prozac* and *Valium* are used, severe training methods, or shocking collars are employed, and abandonment or euthanasia is common, as owners tire of the daily struggle.

Although many dog and cat breeds can be predisposed towards negative behavioral traits, these are more likely to be triggered by chemicals and sugar in the diet, and by early experiences of abandonment or mistreatment. It is obvious that these behaviors are preventable. This is what holistic animal care is all about: to help you support the most positive potential your pet has without the need of force, and thus to prevent or reverse behavioral problems.

UNDERSTANDING YOUR PET'S BEHAVIOR

Many pet owners and veterinarians do not believe that an animal is capable of emotions, although we can see the joy in our pet's eyes when we come home, or their determination to get a command right, or their undying loyalty even in the face of the most adverse responses from their owners. Fear, grief, anger, and mischief are clearly evident from their vocalization, faces, and body language. Understanding your pet's emotions is the first step to understanding their behavior.

THE DOG

Dogs are pack animals who crave close family contact. Love is as vital to them as the air they breathe. If they cannot be near you or are not allowed to live within the family unit, they will seek contact, even negative attention.

Dogs who are left outside or kenneled for the major portion of the day live shorter lives and suffer a higher incidence of behavioral or physical problems. Even if you are away at work, if they have access to both the house and yard, they will feel they are contributing by protecting the family "cave." If you leave them isolated in one area of the house or outside, they will feel banished from the family cave. The resulting stress from this perceived abandonment will affect them, and, whether you notice or not, will eventually manifest as a symptom evident in the pet's behavior.

THE CAT

Cats can be quite difficult to understand at times. If they are isolated, they will demand to be noticed. If they are given attention, they ignore us. Unlike dogs that have a strong urge to "cave" with their human pack, cats seem quite happy spending their time alone. Yet they will experience stress if they feel "abandoned." Cats have more complex needs than other pets. Their relationship to their caregivers can be very different from a dog's. Most of the recommendations in this book will work for both cats and dogs, although there can be vast differences in communication between the two species.

COMMUNICATING WITH YOUR PET

The majority of behavioral problems are created by mis-communication between the caregiver and pet—you are speaking two different languages. Imagine for a moment that you are in a foreign land trying to understand your tour guide who doesn't speak English. What a relief it is when you work out some signals. Pets look to us for such signals, trying to decipher what we want because they desperately want to please us. Begin to understand your dog or cat's behavior by first putting yourself in their paws.

Ask yourself if your pet can rely on:

- Your love—consistent, fair and gentle; focused and sincere
- Your attention—daily regard for their emotional and physical well-being
- Your care—responsive to disorder, accident, or illness, acute or long-term
- Your home—a safe and loving shelter, free of fear or stress
- Your devotion—through the easy, fun times *and* the difficult ones

Exploring and changing certain things to fit your pet's needs, rather than purely your own, can prevent struggle on both your parts. Good communication comes out of safe, consistent behavior from you that your pet can learn to rely upon. Trust can only be developed and maintained if you feel good about each other.

CHOOSING THE RIGHT DOG OR CAT

If you are contemplating a new addition to your family, it is important to consider what type of pet will best suit your personality and needs, as well as your other pets. If you like a tranquil lifestyle, a nervous or high-strung animal is not going to be easy for you to handle. If you are a very active person who wants a pet that will participate with you, then a passive, gentle breed is not the best choice.

If you are a gardener, a Terrier, who is bred to dig, will not be a good choice. A Sheltie dog may be small, but they, like Siamese cats, require a lot of exercise or they can become destructive and very vocal. Both breeds have a reputation for driving owners crazy with their incessant complaints. A Great Dane does not require a lot of exercise, but can be a handful for a senior citizen to train. A Persian cat is gorgeous and Poodles do not shed, but both require a lot of grooming. Research the many breed books available to learn about the feeding, exercise, and care requirements of the breeds that interest you, before you bring home a lifelong partner.

Assess your needs first. Does your family travel a lot? Are you active outdoors? Do you have rambunctious children? A Golden Retriever may be well suited to you. If you prefer a cat, a Main Coon is a better choice than a Siamese. Think of the perfect pet for you, and then investigate the different breeds with those characteristics.

Once you have narrowed your choices down to a few breeds, visit breeders and shelters to look at these pets firsthand. Each individual animal, regardless of breed or genetics, has specific life experiences that result in certain traits.

Just because you picked a Siamese cat, a high-maintenance breed known for their antics, doesn't mean that an individual Siamese cat can't be calm and easy to live with.

If you have received a pet as a gift or already chose one that does not suit your family's lifestyle (the number one cause of behavioral problems is an unwanted pet), do not despair. It may take longer or require more patience, but it is possible for even the most unruly pet to become a functional, loving, family member.

WHEN YOU JUST CAN'T GET ALONG WITH YOUR PET

If you feel that you cannot live with your pet, you may want to find it a new home. Please don't do so without first attempting to guide its behavior. Remember that it is not fair to confine an animal to a home or yard where it is unwelcome. It is not fair for you to await anxiously for the next episode. Many people keep pets for years out of guilt, but they never realize that their pet is also miserable. Is years of emotional abandonment, and frequently of physical abuse, better for a pet than the few months it would take for the animal to settle into a new family?

Feeding, training, and medical care are not enough. Pets bond emotionally with their families. Without this bond a pet's life is empty and wasted, and they will grieve its loss. If you have not bonded with your pet, it may not be your fault or your pet's fault. The animal may be better off with another family and so will you.

TRAINING WITHOUT TRAUMA

Never raise your hand to an animal. They will think that you are attacking them. Most people hit their dog or cat out of the frustration that results from poor communication. Pets learn by repetition. It takes approximately seventy-five repetitions for dogs and fifty repetitions for cats for them to understand and learn what you want. The pet must repeatedly associate the desired behavior with the specific command before they understand and are not simply reacting to you. Unless they understand your command completely, they are likely to disregard a command because they do not associate it with the desired action. Training provides pets with an understanding of your boundaries and their abilities. Proper communication results in successful training and the proper behavior at all times, not only when the leash is on.

The key components to training without trauma are:

- Clear and consistent communication
- Identifiable and consistent boundaries
- Consistent praise or disapproval of your pet's behavior
- Consistent and appropriate action when a time out is needed
- Love, consistency, more love, more consistency, and even more love

It is not difficult to train a dog to understand commands, anticipate and exhibit proper behavior, and to follow obediently. Cats, on the other hand, are often considered untrainable, but this is not necessarily true. Have you have ever watched your cat run to you when you opened a can of cat food? Then you know just how trainable a cat can be. One of my clients told me that her cats knew the difference between the electric can opener she used to open their food and the one she used to open the family's cans. Even though she could not hear any difference between the two can openers, her cats did. They never showed up if the "family" can opener was turned on.

The most important thing to teach your cat or dog is how to be handled properly without fuss. Trained pets should allow themselves to be picked up and held or kenneled indefinitely without stress. Trained pets do not mind being put in pet carriers or riding in a moving vehicle. They do not mind being examined by you or any other person. You must also be able to touch them all over their body and paws, and look inside their ears and mouth. You must be able to examine them carefully if they are ever hurt or ill. If they are not used to being held and examined, if it's necessary to do so, it may do more harm than the injury or illness itself.

Taking the time to train your pet properly will result in a better, more reliable companion. A trained pet is less likely to be destructive, to run off and get hit by a car, to harm another pet or human, or to develop bad habits. And, because your pet is pleasant and fun to be around, you will spend more time with them. Your pets are also less likely to get sick when they receive consistent attention. If they do become ill or injured, they will be calmer and easier to examine, will experience less recovery stress, and will respond more quickly to medical treatment.

NOAH'S THEORY:
TWO OF A KIND ARE BETTER THAN ONE

I believe that dogs or cats should be raised in pairs since they are tribal animals and we, as pack leader and primary friend, are often not available to them. A pair of animals will reduce loneliness, will prevent inappropriate behavior, and will reduce illness. If you have more than two dogs or two cats, you may not have enough of yourself to go around. Never have more dogs or cats than you can pet at the same time.

Remember that getting another animal as a companion for your pet is not a substitute for your love and attention. You will have to care for them both and the more time you give, the greater will be the payoff. You will have two well-behaved dogs or cats, rather than one neurotic one.

If you cannot afford to feed and care for two dogs or cats properly, then don't get a second pet. You will hurt both yourself and your pets. If you do not have a lot of time during the week for your one dog or cat, please consider getting another one so they can have each other for company.

Although dogs and cats get along well together, dogs play dog games. Cats play cat games. Dogs and cats have different time clocks. Cats prefer nighttime play, while dogs are friskiest at dawn and dusk. Some pets prefer to have their human family all to themselves and will resent another pet in the house, but most single pets are starved for company during the long hours their caregivers are away.

The more time and attention you invest in understanding your pet's needs, the easier it will be to prevent behavioral issues. A happy, well-adjusted pet is less likely to suffer from disease, since emotional stress, as well as genetics and diet, can contribute to immune dysfunction and the manifestation of symptoms. A pet who is fed the very best diet and supplements, but lives in a stressful or fearful environment will have trouble assimilating nutrients and maintaining good health. Providing a loving, stable home will help support your animal's well-being as much as anything else you can do.

Behavior Is Influenced by Lifestyle and Diet

The holistic animal care lifestyle addresses the whole body rather than its parts, encompassing the body, mind, spirit, and the environment. The application of various health and behavior modification modalities is done in a synergistic way to help stimulate, strengthen, support, and balance the body's biological processes and the animal's emotions. Emotional stability comes from adjusting the pet's "filter" to lessen negative reactions and encourage good behavior.

Nutrition is central to holistic animal care. It can often be the deciding factor between emotional wellness, good behavioral dynamics, health, and disease or behavioral problems. Poor nutrition will quickly lead to a chemical imbalance, cripple the body's curative abilities, and possibly create behavioral problems. Regardless of the amount of attention, drugs, or natural remedies given pets, if they do not receive adequate nutrition, their own curative response and emotional balance is hindered.

Nutrition is also the cornerstone of a modality known as naturopathy. Defined by a medical dictionary as "a drug-less system of therapy by the use of physical forces, such as air, light, water, heat, massage, etc.," naturopathy emphasizes supporting the body's natural ability to eliminate imbalance. Naturopaths believe that a major cause of disease and negative emotions is an excessive build-up of toxic materials (often due to improper eating and lack of exercise) which clog the eliminatory system. These toxins can irritate the pet's nervous system, triggering inappropriate and destructive reactions. Various techniques are used to detoxify and stimulate the body, so that negative behaviors and other symptoms, even chronic diseases, are reversed. Pets are put on supportive programs of high-quality nutrition, proper food combining (to stimulate and aid digestion), nutritional supplements, and herbs. Emphasis is placed on prevention, which is considered the best cure.

Herbs have been used by every culture since ancient times to stimulate healing. Recently, the potential of herbs as mood stabilizers has been clinically validated. It is widely believed that people began using herbs after observing how animals in the wild instinctively select appropriate herbs when they are ill or under stress. Leaves, roots, bark, flowers, and seeds are used to assist the healing process primarily by helping the body to eliminate and to detoxify. Herbs provide a slower, deeper action than prescription drugs.

Another modality which has a slower, deeper action is homeopathy. Sometimes nutrition or herbs won't be enough—they may begin the cleansing process and support the body (by strengthening it so that it can stabilize itself emotionally and physically), but often it is the homeopathic remedy that can stimulate a deeper level of healing. By addressing and altering the way in which your pet processes information and responds to stimuli (your pet's "filter"), homeopathy can safely and gently address your pet's emotional issues and negative behaviors. For instance, the homeopathic remedies *Aconite* and *Ignatia* can prevent negative behaviors that are caused by trauma. When a pet has experienced a trauma, similar situations can produce the same behavior the next time the pet perceives danger.

The German physician, Samuel Hahnemann, founded homeopathy on one principle that has held true ever since the late 1700s: like cures like—that a substance that can create symptoms can cure them as well. This principle revolutionized the understanding of symptoms and disease.

Hahnemann noted certain similarities between symptoms produced by some diseases and the drugs used to treat them. From this he established his "Law of Similars," which identified the principle that a disease could be cured by whatever medicine produced similar symptoms when given to a healthy person. Homeopathy works with, rather than against, the body's own efforts to regain health.

We know that a bee sting will causes a topical reaction, including swelling, fluid accumulation, redness of the skin, pain, and soreness, a reaction that is intensified by heat or pressure. Some sensitive animals will also experience behavioral symptoms such as apathy, lack of concentration, listlessness, grief, or the opposite, jealousy, rage, whining, and fear. These reactions can cause the pet to cry or whine, to be unable to learn required behaviors, or to cause obsessive behaviors such as stealing or chewing objects.

When a homeopathically prepared dilute solution of the venom (known as Apis) is given to a pet with these symptoms—even if negative emotions or traumatic experiences rather than a bee sting cause them—the condition or behavior will soon be cured. The essential key is that the symptoms are similar to what the remedy, in its undiluted state, would create.

Flower essences (which balance emotional states) and tissue cell salts (which support physiological processes that help stabilize emotions) act similarly, in stimulating the body's own natural healing and homeostasis.

THE HOLISTIC PET

A healthy, holistically reared pet is in a state of balance that exists on three interrelated levels: physical, emotional, and environmental. A healthy pet has physical vitality and is free from physiological malfunction, possesses emotional clarity resulting in good behavior and happiness, and receives (as well as contributes) joy, love, and security in their living environment.

This is the opposite of a chemically reared pet, who is often in a state of imbalance or dis-ease. This animal lacks vitality and suffers from chronic symptoms due to physiological malfunction, displays emotional stress resulting in negative behavior, and often also lives in a physically toxic environment. Since it is impossible to have one biological system affected without affecting the other systems, including the nervous system and, thus, the emotions, a system that is not in balance is more susceptible to assault.

Holistic animal care is simple and safe to use. A healthy pet is a happy pet. *Treat the body well and the body will be well.* By providing the body with sufficient amounts of high-quality food, correct supplements, and holistic modalities when appropriate, the body will remain in a state of balance. If the balanced body is assaulted by certain stresses, which create emotional strain and imbalance, it has the strength to trigger the curative process and reestablish its emotional and physical balance.

THE PROBLEM PET

Some pets who are born genetically compromised develop emotional/behavioral disorders, such as hyper-aggression that can result in biting. Many pets who were not born genetically compromised also suffer from aggression or other negative emotions because they are exposed to chemicals and an emotionally and/or physically toxic environment. Chemicals and environmental stress (such as fear) alter the body's primary biological functions, place undue stress on vital organs and glands necessary for proper immune function, and destroy healthy tissue. Pets who have been challenged emotionally or behaviorally have often been exposed to:

- standard commercial pet foods
- artificial treats
- shotgun medications (the indiscriminate use of "standard" medications)
- excessive vaccinations and yearly boosters
- toxic cleaning and pest-control products (especially collars or monthly drug doses)
- environmental pollution (without the benefit of regular detoxification)
- an emotionally and/or physically stressful living environment (past and present)

Commercial pet diets and treats are the primary reason pets develop all types of poor training responses, including negative emotions, which can cause behavioral problems. It should be noted that the quality of the ingredients can do more harm and are more likely to trigger a response than the ingredients themselves. The standard use of by-products and meat sources unfit for human consumption severely limit the pet's ability to digest and assimilate nutrients well. The use of artificial colors or flavors, chemical preservatives, nitrates, and rancid animal fats also interfere with the nervous system and can trigger behavioral outbursts. Poorly digested matter becomes harder to eliminate, causing a back-up of old fecal material in the bowel, which further prohibits assimilation of vital nutrients needed to reverse neurological or emotional dysfunction.

Pets often aren't given the opportunity to exercise and can't always go outside to move their bowels. A pet fed poor food loaded with chemicals and by-products will not be able to properly digest the food. This undigested matter moves into the colon, but since complete evacuation is not really possible, the fecal matter will line the walls of the colon. Chemicals (such as ethoxyquin, a commonly used pet food preservative that is a moisture prohibitive) limits the lubrication necessary for a properly evacuated stool, and the fecal matter hardens, finally producing small, hard, dry stools.

Many pet food companies will tell you that these stools mean their food is more "digestible with less waste to pick up." What do you think a medical doctor would say to you, if you described your own stools as small, dry lumps? Certainly, a better-quality food will produce less stool volume (generally due to less fillers and better digestibility), but it should not be caused by a lack of moisture in the stool.

As old fecal material builds up inside the colon, it becomes harder and harder for the body to clean out. This interferes with the body's ability to absorb or "ventilate" nutrients from digested matter in the colon into the bloodstream for distribution among the body's hungry cells and energy-depleted organ systems.

The harder the ingredients are to break down and process, and the more chemicals that are present, the more stress is placed on the body's ability to function properly. The harder the body has to work, the quicker it breaks down and falls apart. Due to improper digestion and assimilation, the body lacks the resources to utilize whatever nutrients it receives. These nutrients are vital to proper biological processes such as the immune system. Improper digestion and assimilation also leads to a build-up of general waste (toxins), which places a huge burden upon the eliminatory organs. As the liver and kidneys become burdened, the body attempts to detoxify through the largest eliminatory organ it has, the skin. Hence, the development of skin and coat problems in pets who display behavioral or neurological problems. Additionally, the lymphatic and endocrine systems are over-stimulated, possibly leading to the development of a deeper, more serious disease like cancer.

HOW DIET AFFECTS BEHAVIOR

The primary line of defense in preventing or treating behavioral problems is a sound nutritional program. Your pet's diet should consist of fresh, high-quality ingredients that are easy to digest and assimilate. Home cooking is optimal, but might not be practical for you. Therefore, you must be very careful to seek out a quality commercial product. Become an educated label reader. Look beyond catchy terms such as "natural," "organic," "healthy," "symptom-related diet," and "human-grade quality." Ask the manufacturer directly to prove their quality and guarantee their formula.

Seek out only Grade A or B meats (human grade). Avoid the four-D meats: dead, dying, diseased, or disabled animals not fit for human consumption. Four-D meats are the meats most commonly used in pet foods. Grain by-products also present a big problem in commercial pet products. Wheat millings, brewer's rice (leftovers from brewing), and flour are inexpensive fillers devoid of nutritional value that can severely compromise your pet's health. Often these grains are purchased rancid and moldy (to save money), adding the possibility of a toxic reaction which could alter your animal's brain chemistry and trigger negative emotions. Grade 1 or 2 grains (all human grades) should be used, preferably whole ground, to ensure their nutritional goodness. Go for the best quality you can afford—think of it as an insurance policy against poor health and future expenses.

Beware of "lite" diets—they may cause weight gain and a sense of starvation. Fillers may be filling, but they are devoid of nutrients. Many pets on lite or excessively fiber-rich diets feel hungry all the time. They cannot concentrate and may become nervous or aggressive. The brain decides if there is enough nutrition available, regardless of the diet, and stores calories to ward off starvation. A properly balanced, quality diet that provides easy to assimilate nutrients will bring your animals to their proper weight and help to balance their emotions.

People are often concerned that changing their pet's diet will result in digestive upsets. This is true, if you are changing between one poor-quality or chemical-based diet to another! When switching to a healthier, more natural diet, there should be no irritating ingredients to upset the balance. Often, the biggest problems during the transition are soft stool and gas, due to the fact that you probably are overfeeding your pet on the new diet.

One cup of a grocery store food is full of filler, almost fifty percent. When you switch to a higher-quality food, there is generally less filler. Therefore, feeding the same quantities (cup for cup) will result in overfeeding and gastric upset. Overfeeding can make your pet lazy and unresponsive. Read and follow the manufacturer's specific recommendations for the new diet and then watch your pets carefully for the first few weeks to see how they react.

Overfeeding often occurs when people begin cooking for their pets. I suggest that you seek a well-researched book on natural pet care that includes recipes for home-cooked diets.

I recommend that you don't feed your pet raw meat. Although this is now becoming common, I have encountered many sick animals who have been fed such a diet. I believe that animals evolve to fit their environment, and since our pets have been domesticated for so long, they have changed into processed food eaters. They have lost the ability to digest raw meat tissue, bone, hide, feathers, etc., on a regular basis. Many pets can become aggressive or develop other behavioral issues when they have been fed raw meats or other improperly balanced high-protein diets.

Even with the use of digestive enzymes, I still see most pets struggling to digest raw animal tissue or high-protein diets. Don't get me wrong—I prefer home-cooked foods to commercially processed pet foods. Lightly cooking meat (which does not destroy enzymes and nutrients) helps to break it down so that it is easier to digest. Poor-quality or high-meat protein diets increase urea, a waste product of meat metabolism, which is a known nervous system irritant. Frequently, meat has not been properly handled and can pass *e. coli* bacteria or parasites to the pet, leading to gastrointestinal distress and mood changes.

I should emphasize that, even with the best-quality, balanced diet (using cooked or raw meats), nutritional supplementation is presently necessary to provide many nutrients now missing from our food chain. For instance, some research indicates that fifty years ago spinach had up to eighty percent more nutritional values than today! This is true (in varying degrees) for other vegetables, grains, and fruits, as well as meats from animals fed off the land. Our earth has been stripped of many naturally occurring micronutrients, which used to be found in soil. Our vegetables are only as good as the soil they grow in. Years of over-farming, the use of toxic chemicals or fertilizers, and environmental pollution such as acid rain have taken their toll.

Even organic farming methods cannot guarantee that the produce will be more nutritious, as it will take approximately seventy-five years before the nutrients return to the soil. Therefore, it is important to supplement our animal's (and our own) diets to ensure that we receive the fundamental nutrients required. Even pet foods which are "nutritionally complete" according to AAFCO (American

Association of Feed Control Officers) guidelines aren't complete according to what is truly needed for basic good physical and emotional health. For instance, the guidelines allow so much protein per cup of food, but that protein does not have to be *digestible*, therefore, it cannot be assimilated as protein! The same holds true for certain sources of Vitamin A or calcium, to name a few! Vitamin B complex, which is vital for proper nervous system and brain chemistry function, is not required by law to be included in commercial feeds. The few available B vitamins in feeds are often provided by brewer's yeast, which seems to trigger negative emotions. Therefore, proper nutrition not only includes quality, easy to digest foods, but also the appropriate supplementation to support optimum emotional health, while stimulating your pet's curative potential.

These are the key ingredients for a healthy diet:

- Fresh ingredients with no unpleasant odor (indicating rancidity)
- Whole foods such as whole-ground grains, not "flours," "mill runs," or "by-products"
- Concentrated protein sources known as "meal" (as in "lamb meal" or "beef meal") are preferred over whole meats (listed only as "lamb"). This is not to be confused with "by-product meal." (See list of ingredients to avoid.)

The term "meal" refers to the process of removing up to eighty percent, but no less than forty-five percent, of the ingredient's natural water content, so there is more meat protein for your money (since water only adds to the ingredients' weight). The ingredients are listed on the label by weight with the heaviest ingredient first. For instance, it is deceiving to see chicken listed first when the majority of the protein in the pet food is derived from grains, not animal protein. This type of formula greatly reduces the cost of ingredients for the manufacturer.

Because one pound of meal is equivalent to approximately three pounds of whole meat, and there is an additional charge to dehydrate the meat, meal is expensive to produce. Therefore, many companies use the meat to draw you to the label, but use a cheaper ingredient for the actual protein—one that may trigger allergies, which can result in mood disorders. This is true for all chicken, turkey, rabbit, fish, and other animal protein sources used in commercial pet foods.

Look for the following ingredients on your pet food label:

- Identifiable, digestible animal protein or fat sources such as beef, beef meal, lamb, lamb meal, lamb fat, chicken, chicken meal or chicken fats, turkey, ostrich, etc., not vague terms like "meats," "poultry," or "animal fats"

- USDA Grade A or B animal protein sources, preferably raised without growth hormones or recently given antibiotics (both are suspected triggers of aggression in pets)

- USDA Grade 1 or 2 whole grains preferably free of chemical pesticides or herbicides. Organic grains are not cost-effective in commercial pet foods. If the label on the food you are feeding your pet reads "organic," demand written certification. However, "pesticide-free" is available, or "washed" grains are possible. For home-cooked diets, go for the best ingredients you can afford!

- Balanced, combined ingredients of proteins and grain sources seem to suit most pets better than single-source ingredients, contrary to popular belief.

- Vegetable and fruit fiber should be present (for example, carrots and apples) for proper digestion, natural flavoring, and trace nutrients. Fiber in general is very important for proper elimination. Moreover, fiber (provided in whole grains) is full of vital nutrients.

- Quality sources of fat (necessary for energy and good coats) such as vegetable or fish oils, rather than animal fats, should be used for dogs, especially hyperactive dogs. Vegetable and fish oils provide energy and fatty acids without the toxicity of many animal fats, which is a major trigger of negative emotions and confusion. Cats, on the other hand, need the higher level of energy provided by animal fats. Cats on fat-free or calorie-restricted diets often develop behavioral issues as a result of too little energy.

- Remember that you generally get what you pay for! If you pay $10.00 for a forty-pound bag, and the cost of making and marketing the food is as follows: paper bag 85 cents, shipping $1.00, advertising and handling 75 cents, yielding a $2.50 profit for the manufacturer, $1.25 for the wholesaler, and a $2.25 for the retailer—how much do you think the manufacturer actually spent on the ingredients?

- Take into consideration how much cheaper food you will need to sustain your pet. Often, the cheaper foods will prove to be more expensive, because you have to use so much more food than you would with a better-quality diet, which contains less filler.

- Product should be fresh when purchased. If you bought fresh-baked bread, it would still be wonderful to eat the next day, but would you still be eating it two weeks later? Be sure to check the date the food was packed. Never use food (especially naturally preserved diets) that is older than six months, unless it is packaged in a completely sealed, airtight, barrier bag. Stale food has not only lost its flavor, but also most of its nutritional value through oxidation, and your pet will not enjoy it.

- Eating should be rewarding both physically and emotionally! A pet that does not feel satisfied will be distracted by his hunger, will become depressed when fed the same poor-tasting food day after day, and will beg for other, more nutritious and tasty foods.

These are ingredients to avoid in a healthy diet:

- Chemical preservatives: Ethoxyquin, BHA and/or BHT, Propylene Glycol, Nitrates
- Artificial flavors or colors, which are suspected of triggering hyperactivity, aggression, and confusion

- Foul-smelling ingredients must be avoided. If traditional pet food, even in fresh bags, smells rancid, throw it out. When pets don't like what they are fed, depressive or aggressive behavior can occur.

- Greasy food, that leaves smelly oil on the bag or a sheen on canned formulas, indicates that it is heavy in animal fats or tallow (rendered carcasses and recycled cooking grease from restaurants). These are difficult to digest and are most often rancid prior to manufacturing. This accounts for that rancid "pet food" smell, even in "fresh" bags. Rancid food can be irritating to both the nervous system and the liver and can cause negative reactions.

- Animal by-products such as "beef by-product," "lamb by-product," "chicken by-product" (a mixture of the whole carcass including feces, cancerous tumors, hide, hooves, beaks, feathers, and fur). Also avoid their mysterious cousins: "meat" or "meat by-products" (a mixture of whatever mammals, including road kill, rats, and other dogs and cats ground together), "fish by-product," and "poultry by-products" (a mixture of whatever feathered animals got ground up together, including pigeons)—Need I say more?

- Grain by-products ("mill runs," "flours," "middlings," "husks," and "parts") should be avoided at all costs. Not only have all their nutritionally rich parts been removed, they may irritate the digestive and eliminatory tracts. These grain by-products are cheap fillers used as a protein source (although they cannot be digested and therefore cannot be assimilated) to increase the finished product's weight and mass.

- Soybeans—dogs cannot digest them. Canine digestion lacks an amino acid necessary to digest soybeans. Because tofu and soybean oil are already processed many dogs can tolerate them. However, most pet foods contain soybean meal or husks that can trigger bloat, an often-fatal digestive reaction. Soybeans can also produce hyperactivity or fear in some dogs. Cats can thrive on soybeans in any form, especially soybean meal, which is high in fat and available energy. Cats require the amino acid Taurine that is derived from meat and when they lack Taurine it can lead to many behavioral issues.

- Fillers such as powdered "cellulose," or "cellulose fiber" can include recycled newspaper, sawdust, and cardboard. "Plant cellulose" usually refers to ground peanut hulls, which are very damaging to sensitive colon tissues and interfere with assimilation. Beet pulp or grain by-products have no nutritional value, but do add bulk and weight to the finished product.

- Yeast is a cheap source of B Vitamins, amino acids, and some nutrients. It also adds natural flavor and color. It is touted for flea control and a shiny coat, but yeast can contribute to negative emotions by burdening the liver and interfering in proper digestion. A common feline reaction to yeast is the hyper twitching and jumping that can suddenly overcome even the calmest cats. These reactions are quickly reversed after yeast is removed from the diet. Yeast can cause hyperactivity, nervousness, and aggression in dogs.

- Sugar is added to most commercial diets and treats. It is found on the label as "sucrose," "beet pulp," "molasses," "cane syrup," "fruit solids," and, of course, "sugar." It is a very cheap and heavy filler, and is addictive. Additional sugar in the diet is the primary trigger of weight problems, diabetic conditions, and behavioral problems in pets today. Hyperactivity, aggression, learning difficulties, and fear biting are just a few of the behavioral issues triggered by sugar.

I recommend supplementing the food you feed your pet (no matter how good it is) with a well-balanced vitamin and mineral supplement. Seek out a high-quality, high-potency daily multiple. Food-source supplements are excellent choices for the general maintenance of healthy dogs and cats, but they are not potent enough to prevent or reverse significant disease in a genetically compromised or chronically ill pet. Be sure that you provide at least the minimum requirements of vital nutrients, because, for whatever reason, your pet may not be able to assimilate its food completely. It is additional insurance. I recommend these nutrients daily, based on a cat or average twenty-five-pound dog:

- *Vitamin A* for a strong immune system, eyes, tissue repairs — 2,500 mg.
- *Beta Carotene* supports Vitamin A assimilation — 1,200 mg.
- *Vitamin B1* for energy, the primary B for emotional well-being and intelligence — 25 mg.
- *Vitamin B2* necessary for fat and carbohydrate metabolism; promotes clear thinking — 25 mg.
- *Vitamin B6* for red blood cell production, protein metabolism, hyperirritability — 25 mg.
- *Vitamin B12* aids in calcium absorption, anti-inflammatory; forms myelin sheath — 25 mcg.
- *Niacin* promotes healthy skin and nerves, supports digestion, reversal of dementia — 25 mg.
- *Pantothenic Acid* is an antioxidant vital for adrenal activity; supports brain function — 25 mg.
- *Folic Acid* necessary for DNA, enzyme efficiency, and blood — 100 mcg.
- *Choline*, a vital neurotransmitter; works with Inositol to emulsify fats; reverses brain disease — 25 mg.
- *Inositol* lowers fatty deposits in the liver, controls cholesterol, enhances oxygen to brain — 25 mg.
- *PABA* protects skin from sun-related cancer, supports coat color — 25 mg.
- *Biotin* metabolism of fatty acids and amino acids, makes antibodies — 25 mcg.
- *Vitamin C* repairs connective tissue, builds resistance to cancer and stress — 75 mg.
- *Vitamin D* promotes a sense of well-being— the sunshine vitamin; helps reduce fear — 200 IU.
- *Calcium* needed for strong bones and teeth, reduces muscular stress — 12 mg.
- *Phosphorus* supports structure, oxygen to the brain, maintains pH — 5 mg.
- *Magnesium* critical for bones, nerve, and muscle function; helps relax pets — 2 mg.
- *Potassium* supports electrolyte and pH balance, neurotransmitter; reduces hyperactivity — 2.5 mg.

- *Iron* combines with copper and proteins to form red blood cells — 4.5 mg.
- *Manganese* nourishes the brain, nerves; supports SOD/antioxidant — 1.5 mg.
- *Zinc* co-enzyme of SOD—protects against free radicals/cancer — 4 mg.
- *Iodine* is vital to proper thyroid function and proper metabolism — 35 mcg.
- *Copper* for inflammatory response, bone mineralization, coat color — 75 mcg.
- *Glutamic Acid* supports nerve health, metabolizes fats and sugars — 6 mg.
- *Selenium* and *Chromium* are immune and emotional health minerals — 6 mcg.

To introduce a dietary change and to kick off a successful program for the prevention or rehabilitation of emotional issues that result in behavioral problems, begin by imposing a short twenty-four-hour period of fasting.

Many people associate fasting with enforced starvation. This couldn't be further from the truth—fasting can save your dog or cat's life! Fasting encourages the body to detoxify and re-balance. The fasting methods I recommend are very safe and gentle.

To avoid the pleading look that pets (especially dogs) give you during fasting, do something fun with your pet, at their usual dinnertime. Bring home a new toy (but not out of guilt!) or take your friend out for a fifteen-minute walk. Not only will these activities occupy you and your pet's thoughts but they also will provide much-needed exercise.

A short twenty-four hour fast with homeopathic support can make a world of difference in your pet's health and behavior. During fasting, old fecal material is expelled from the colon while vital eliminatory organs, the kidneys and liver, are given a break from processing daily waste. This allows a deeper processing of backed-up toxins and a rebalancing of biochemical influences, resulting in improved digestive and eliminatory systems. These are necessary for the intake of both nutrients and therapeutic substances (as found in herbs), which will help strengthen the immune system and build resistance to negative emotions. The reduction of toxins in the body also improves the overall condition of the pet, often enough to reverse most symptoms. The more obvious symptoms of negative emotions often begin to improve following a short fast. The pet will become calmer and more responsive.

Usually within the first six to eight weeks after detoxification, you will see a reversal of physical symptoms, such as a poor coat and a better disposition. Seventy-five percent of pets will improve quickly after detoxification, dietary changes, and proper supplementation. In the remaining twenty-five percent of cases, including those with true allergies or chronic debilitating dis-ease that may be triggering the behavior, the judicious use of homeopathic, herbal, and nutritional supplementation in a continuing course of treatment will definitely strengthen the animal's constitution. This will ultimately reduce or eliminate their negative emotions as well as improve their behavior. With chronic cases, it can often take several weeks to a year to eliminate the symptoms or reverse negative emotions. Bear in mind that you are attempting to change the way your pet perceives the world (through their filter) and that in order to reprogram that filter, it may take more than one course of action.

Simply suppressing behaviors pharmaceutically may not work or may lead to premature death. Year after year of toxins attacking a body—protected by a struggling immune system—will only serve to weaken the body further. A sound nutritional program supported with ongoing detoxification, proper supplementation, and rebalancing with homeopathic remedies or herbs, while avoiding (or at least limiting) vaccination boosters, chemicals, and drugs, is the best way to strengthen your pet's immune system, thereby improving his health and happiness.

There are gentle and effective ways to trigger the body's eliminatory systems (the colon, kidneys, liver, lungs, skin, and lymph system) to process waste removal on a deeper level than is required for daily maintenance. By utilizing fasting, you will be giving your animal a jump-start on not only preventing behavioral issues—but reversing and possibly eliminating, negative emotions.

OTHER FACTORS THAT CREATE EMOTIONAL IMBALANCE

A pet may be exposed to chemicals and irritants in non-dietary, forms. Chemicals can affect the nervous system, increase chronic pain or disease, and make the pet feel weak and irritable. Whether the irritant is a chemical-based breath mint, an annual vaccination booster, an artificially perfumed shampoo, medicated skin treatments, flea or tick control products, household cleaning agents, or long-term medication, any or all can have an effect on your animal's emotional health. Think of the healthy, emotionally stable body as a balanced scale. If you keep adding these chemicals to one side, the scale remains out of balance. But if you add good nutrition and minimize the build-up of chemicals on the other side, this scale will stay in balance.

It is important to address other factors that may cause imbalance. Structural imbalances can often be a primary cause of behavioral problems. Old injuries or genetic malfunctions, such as rheumatoid arthritis, can place stress on certain organ systems and contribute to pain and fatigue. A build-up of calcium deposits and joint or spinal inflammation may put pressure on the nervous system or the digestive organs such as the stomach. This pressure can interfere with the normal function of the stomach, causing improper digestion and assimilation of nutrients. It also disrupts nerve impulses resulting in negative behavior. Often, addressing these structural problems will help to reverse behavioral issues. Chiropractic adjustments, massage, acupressure, and acupuncture can help you address your animal's emotional issues. Remember that antibiotics, pain medication, or anti-inflammatory drugs can cause aggression, nervousness, or depression.

Another factor that can cause imbalance and lead to behavioral problems is a stressful environment. Have you ever "felt butterflies in your stomach" and experienced a loose bowel due to a stressful situation? Pets who experience extreme emotions (fear, nervousness, and tension) are more likely to exhibit inappropriate behaviors. Abandonment (physical or emotional), harsh training or wrong disciplining, and lack of exercise or play often trigger negative reactions. Pets do not forget earlier traumatic experiences, including chronic illness or a slow recovery from injury. Their emotional responses are altered by each traumatic experience, which results in negative reactions.

Pets can experience digestive problems and glandular imbalances due to chronic stress, which may exacerbate emotional issues and behavioral problems. Sources of stress include family changes such as relocation, members leaving or dying, divorce or new births, new jobs, etc. The pituitary, adrenal, and thyroid glands may be injured by chronic emotional or physical stress. These glands are associated with the fight-or-flight reaction to negative stimuli. Excessive adrenaline production will increase nervous or fearful emotions, including aggression. A safe and nurturing environment will ensure your pet's emotional well-being. The use of nutritional supplementation and remedies, especially flower essences, to re-balance the emotions, can often be the key to emotional stability.

When an animal is out of balance, waste builds up not only in the colon but also in the bloodstream, nervous system, joints, and eliminatory organs. Urea, a waste product of meat protein metabolism, can cause negative emotions and behavioral problems. It also accounts for the high number of pets who test positive for meat allergies, common in pets with severe emotional issues. Many behavioral problems also occur in pets that suffer from allergies or arthritis. The poorer the quality of meat, and the more difficult it is to digest, the more waste is produced. Urea toxicity manifests itself through certain, notable symptoms:

- behavioral problems including obsession, confusion, poor memory, aggression, nervousness, and fear
- premature aging with chronic arthritic or allergic symptoms and organ disease
- known or suspected allergies to beef, pork, meat, meat by-products, or meat meal
- excessive licking and chewing of paws, resulting in edema and lick granuloma; licking can become compulsive
- prickly heat-type rashes, itchy skin, with or without small pimples or pustules
- excessive loss of hair or coat condition, often in response to a stressful situation
- foul-smelling breath, flatulence, and/or stool
- increased fatty tumor, cyst, or cancerous tumor production
- liver, pancreatic, gall bladder, and kidney dysfunction
- weakened immune responses, especially chronic skin infections
- parasitic infestation, especially fleas and ticks (which feed off of skin-eliminated waste)
- neurological issues, including seizures and tumors of the brain or spinal cord

Yeast is another nasty ingredient found in most commercial pet diets, treats, supplements, flea and tick control products, and even many pet medications, including calming formulas. Yeast, which is noted for its anti-flea and tick properties, is in practically everything! A cheap filler ingredient, it does provide some B vitamins, minerals, amino acids, and natural flavor, but it is mostly used to increase the product's volume.

Brewer's yeast, the most common form of yeast in animal foods and other products, is a waste product with most of its nutrients removed during the brewing process. Nutritional yeast, a cultivated product, is nutritionally superior to brewer's yeast and tastier, but it still is not the best source of nutrients and, like brewer's yeast, can be difficult to digest. Adequate levels of B vitamins, which can help reverse many behavioral problems, especially nervousness and hyperactivity, are available only through supplements. Excessive yeast clogs the liver and increases general toxicity. According to recent veterinary findings, animals who suffer from behavior problems are more likely to be allergic to yeast than they are to other food sources of B vitamins. Yeast supplementation, prescribed by veterinarians and alternative practitioners, may initially improve a pet's attitude and behavior, but over a long period of time may cause behavioral problems. A daily multiple vitamin/mineral supplement (high in B complex and Vitamin C), rather than yeast supplementation, can help resolve negative behaviors quickly.

Yeast toxicity manifests itself in symptoms that include:

- aggression, hyperactivity, concentration problems, or fearful behavior in certain pets
- premature aging with arthritic manifestation and possibly digestive symptoms

- known or suspected allergies to yeast or yeast-containing foods such as dry kibble
- ear infections, eye discharges, and upper respiratory problems, including asthma
- excessive licking and chewing of the body and face-rubbing
- hot spots, itchy skin, with or without small pimples or pustules
- slower healing of tissue, including ligaments
- excessive loss of fur or coat condition
- foul-smelling breath, flatulence, and/or stool (especially off-colored stools with mucus)
- increased fatty tumor, cyst, or cancerous tumor production
- poor digestion and assimilation of other nutrients
- blood sugar instability
- high levels of liver enzymes and eosinophils (diagnostic of a damaged liver)
- liver, spleen, gall bladder, and/or pancreatic dysfunction including diabetes
- weakened immune response, especially chronic infections
- increased sensitivities to pollution, vaccinations, and chemicals in general
- parasitic infestation, especially fleas and ticks (which feed off of skin-eliminated waste)

Research on flea and tick infestations has determined that garlic is more powerful as an anti-parasitic agent than yeast. When garlic is combined with yeast, it is less powerful. A clean diet greatly reduces the waste eliminated through the skin. This waste attracts fleas or ticks to the body and then feeds them. Old fecal material in the colon also attracts and feeds internal parasites such as worms. Parasites can account for negative emotions and behavioral changes. Fleas, ticks, and flies can literally drive a pet crazy. Chronic parasitic infestation, including fungal or bacterial mycoses (such as Valley Fever or Tick Fever) and intestinal worms will weaken, confuse, and depress an animal. If you suspect that a physical condition may be the cause of behavioral problems, consult your veterinarian.

As urea, metabolized yeast, and other waste builds up in the body, undue stress is placed upon the nervous system and vital organs, and the body may begin to break down emotionally and physically. First, the ability to break down ingredients is reduced, waste begins to circulate, and fewer nutrients are available to stimulate the body's own defenses. Next the eliminatory, lymphatic, and immune systems begin to break down. Chronic symptoms develop and pharmaceutical or holistic suppression of symptoms is initiated. Once medication is stopped the symptoms return and the cycle continues. Ultimately, there is organ and gland malfunction, possibly leading to an early death. Continued stress and discomfort results in hormonal dysfunction, irritation, and ultimately, behavioral problems.

When an animal begins to exhibit negative emotions and displays behavior problems, the chronic use of medications may be the cause. Steroids can trigger aggression or withdrawal as well as changes in eating and sleeping habits. Antihistamines can make some pets confused and nonresponsive to commands, while other pets may become hyperactive. Thyroid medications can create irrational fear, and antibiotics can make a pet nervous. If your pet's behavioral issues have suddenly appeared, consult your veterinarian to rule out drug interaction as well as injury or illness.

Any pet who displays emotional reactions, and those pets who suffer from neurological or hormonal disorders, chronic disease, old age, or injury can benefit from holistic animal care. Regardless of the emotional issues and behavioral dynamics, the underlying causes are fundamentally the same. A wholesome, toxin-free approach to diet and lifestyle not only can help maintain emotional stability but also can prevent negative emotions from developing.

Training Your Pet
as Nature Intended

TRAINING EQUIPMENT FOR YOUR DOG OR CAT

To train your dog or cat without trauma, the correct training equipment is as important as the correct attitude. When you want to reinforce the boundaries you have established for your pet, using restraint to frustrate your pet briefly (without inflicting physical or emotional pain) is vital. Choosing appropriate equipment can prevent physical trauma during training. Improper use of a collar can choke your pet and cause a sore neck. Your pet may feel frustrated and fearful, and it will be even harder for her to behave correctly. Purchase a harness and leash suitable for the type and size of your animal and for the activities you will be engaged in together. A harness is superior to a collar because it is less likely to cause physical trauma. It also is easier to control your pet. Collars (leather, nylon, or chain) can cause neck trauma and misalignment, can damage the trachea, or can frighten the pet who might succeed in slipping out of the collar.

Once a pet has a negative experience, that experience is imprinted and influences how your pet perceives similar actions in the future. Each time you tug on the leash his urge will be to pull until he can slip out of the collar to regain freedom by force and dominate you, rather than learn to cooperate and receive freedom as a reward.

For identification purposes, tags with both your name and your pet's name, address, and phone number should be secured on a collar that your pet wears at all times. Since a harness can be uncomfortable during rest, and many areas require license tags, a collar may be necessary, but should not be used primarily for restraint.

Be sure to purchase a break-a-way collar, made specifically for cats. Cats, especially those who play outside, can become caught on a fence and choke to death if their collar does not release. Some people like to put a bell on a cat's collar to warn birds, but this can increase the possibility of entanglement. Securing a bell to a harness works great for a cat or even a dog.

Your pet's harness should be snug, but not restrain their movement or breathing. Figure eight harnesses work well on cats or small dogs, while H-shaped halters that fit around and in front of the chest help secure medium- to large-sized dogs. I prefer nylon harnesses to leather, since they weigh less and are cooler. Leather should be used if chewing is a problem or stronger material is needed to secure the animal. Buckles, rather than loops or buttons, should be made of either the high-quality plastic used in camping equipment, or metal.

For a difficult dog, use a facial harness, which controls the movement of a dog's head and the direction of the body. A dog in a facial harness cannot lunge forward or run away because the harness allows them to be turned in a circle. They can fight a collar or harness by leveraging their body against it, but can only follow where their heads go. There is not enough momentum to control the movement of their heads when you use a facial collar.

Use this type of control instead of the pronged or pinch collar. A pinch collar has little spikes inside the collar that pinch the skin of the dog's neck as punishment. A pinch collar also cuts off the dog's air more efficiently than choke chains, which will stop the dog from lunging in an attempt to regain his breath and avoid pain. It is easy to see why this type of collar creates deeply frustrated, unhappy dogs, actually creating more behavioral problems.

If your dog is unresponsive to the harness, you can use a harness to control the dog's movement and a choke-chain collar for correction. With this combination, you can control the body with the harness and gently pull back on the collar for correction without jerking the head or placing pressure on the vertebrae in your dog's neck. Your control becomes a reprimand rather than a punishment.

You can train your cats more efficiently with a harness rather than a collar, because most cats can slip out of a collar easily. With a harness your cat can get fresh air and exercise.

The type of lead you use is also important. A lead that is too heavy, slippery, or bulky will interfere with your control. You should have two leads for your dog. For training and exercise use a lead that is twenty to thirty feet long, made of cotton or nylon webbing with a looped handle at your end and a secure snap on a swivel at the dog's end. A swivel snap will help prevent the lead from tangling as the dog runs and jumps. Choose the narrowest webbing you can for the dog's size to reduce weight and drag on the lead. For better control on larger dogs when moving in and out of traffic or congested areas, a "traffic lead" works well. This lead has a short, heavy looped handle attached to a swivel snap that extends about six inches from the collar. A combination lead is available that is six feet long with a heavy handle at the end and a traffic handle in the middle. This lead works well for bigger dogs whom you'd want to give more freedom.

For smaller dogs and cats, a narrow four or six foot lead works best. Smaller pets are more easily entangled in their tether. Therefore they should be enclosed in a secure area rather than tied up for extended periods, especially with no supervision.

Choose and introduce your collars, harnesses, and leashes carefully. They will help you to handle your dog or cat properly. A well-restrained pet is more likely to pay attention to you and learn more quickly. Good communication reduces errors and negative emotions, and will reduce the likelihood of trauma during training.

The correct way to train with a harness instead of a collar is to guide your pet's movement and establish boundaries, rather than punish or yank your pet back until he complies with your command. Animals want to please their handlers. The only time they will fight the leash is when they do not understand what you want or are afraid to do what you are asking of them.

A pet must be sufficiently comfortable in his harness and lead so that the equipment is not a distraction during training. Since cats will rub their heads against our armpits and dogs often like to nuzzle us there (because it is a prime scent area that pets associate with humans), use your scent to help focus your dog or cat. Rub the harness between your hands and under your armpits. Your pet will associate this piece of equipment with you, which will encourage her to respond to the harness more quickly. It also will reduce any strong smells on the harness. Rub the harness over the animal and make the experience a pleasurable one by verbally soothing and rewarding your animal. Do not force them or chastise them. Pull away quietly if they become too agitated. You want the training to be a good experience.

Slowly introduce the harness even if just to lay it next to the animal at first. As the pet relaxes, rub it over his body allowing him to sniff at it. Put the harness on for a few minutes while praising him. The next day, start again, but this time leave it on for an hour or more.

On the third day, introduce the lead in the same way you introduced the harness. Hold the lead without controlling your pet's movement, and allow your pet to drag it around. Be especially careful during this phase of training that your pet does not get tangled up. Once your pet is comfortable with the lead, you can gently pull it to one side while encouraging them to follow you. Soon they will get used to the lead and no longer fight you. When your pet accepts the harness and lead, formal training can begin.

USING FREEDOM AS A REWARD

Your pet's greatest reward is freedom, but that does not mean allowing her to run away. To a pet, freedom is the ability to interact freely with the family and be loved. If pets are allowed to roam or fight your restraining system, whether it is a collar or harness, they are not concentrating on your commands and the movements required of them to receive their reward—freedom with praise.

Advance training without trauma does not use any form of control other than the trainer's attitude and the pet's obedience (understanding). Once the pet has learned that she will receive rewards and freedom when she stays close to you and responds to commands, advanced training, known as working the pet "off lead," can be employed. A well-trained dog or cat, who has learned to obey without the lead, is trustworthy in everyday situations such as walking outside in open areas or in traffic. I start the training of my kittens or puppies without a lead. I train them with my attitude and control their movements (freedom) with my movements. They are put on a leash only when we go to places that require them. This is mostly for their safety.

Controlling the animal's movements with your own is easy to do, since animals want to have close contact with us

—they need to follow a leader. Certainly, when your pet has been ignored, he will seek attention by showing his independence and challenging you. But a pet that is not emotionally traumatized will want to maintain contact with you.

Turn your back to a dog and ignore him, and he will come to you. Chase after him and he will run away, since the chase is common form of play for dogs. Often a dog's playing is misunderstood and reprimanded by the trainer, when, in fact, it indicates that the dog is responding to you and trying to engage you. Dogs and cats hate to be ignored; therefore, ignoring them is an effective way to punish them. Stop playing with cats and they will swat at your hands begging for more contact. The pet that runs off and ignores you is one who is not emotionally bonded to his leader, his home, or his family. Or the pet is experiencing an extreme emotional response such as fear, or is confused.

GOOD COMMUNICATION IS THE KEY TO SUCCESSFUL TRAINING

Training need not be a difficult process, if your animals understand what is expected of them. The highest failure rate occurs in human/pet teams who cannot communicate properly or understand each other. Miscommunication triggers negative emotions, resulting in behavioral problems. How well you communicate your intentions is critical to successful training. It is easy to lavish praise on a pet for good behavior. However, the way you punish a pet is very important. You must do so without inflicting pain or emotional damage in order to prevent and reverse unwanted behaviors. Understanding how a pet perceives your actions and knowing when the pet needs guidance or discipline is essential.

Be absolutely clear and consistent in your signals:

- Use the same command consistently. Do not say "shoo" one time and "get away" the next.
- Get your pet's attention. Clap your hands or shoot them with a spray of water to break their negative behavior at the moment it happens.
- Give a warning "No!" If the behavior does not change, say "No" in a deeper voice with more growl-tones and mean it. If you use "No" indiscriminately, your pet will become deaf to it.

Disciplining your dog

If the first warning does not produce results, do the following:

- As a second warning, grab the collar or loose jowl skin, and tug lightly to get their attention or reprimand them.
- As a third and final warning, roll them onto their backs by the collar or jowl skin and pin them into submission for ten seconds (count it off). Breaking eye contact is a sign of submission, so, if your dog looks away, you have made your point and can let her go. If they challenge you by staring at you or trying to bite you, then push them down again with a deeper tone of disappointment. If you keep your arm and hand close to the side of the dog's mouth, they are less likely to grab you. It should not take more than three warnings to improve your pet's behavior.
- If negative behavior escalates, isolate the dog in a quiet place for no longer than fifteen minutes. If you isolate your dog for a longer time, they will forget they were "banished." After fifteen minutes, allow them to return without fanfare. After their return, give your dog a command that is easy and praise them for doing it. This will reinforce the benefits of behaving in the pet's mind, and encourage proper behavior the next time.

This method of punishment resembles how a bitch disciplines her pups. Since this form of punishment is familiar, they will understand that their actions are not acceptable. You won't have to chase, scream, hit, or ignore them.

Disciplining your cat

If the first warning does not work for your cat, do the following:

- As a second warning, grab the loose skin on the back of neck, with slight tug. This method should be used immediately if biting or scratching is involved. Also, keeping your fingers, hand, or arm in the cat's mouth, until they try to get away, will quickly take the fun out of "attacking" you. It won't hurt your cat, just frustrate her. Your cat will stop the unwanted behavior to regain freedom.

- As a third and final warning—only if needed for discipline— restrain your cat by holding him by the collar or loose skin for ten seconds (count it off). Don't let them move. Cats hate being held back in this way. They will quickly do what you want.

- If the negative behavior escalates, isolate the cat in a quiet place for no longer than fifteen minutes. If longer than that time, they will forget they were "banished" and begin to feel abandoned. Allow them to return without fanfare and quickly find a good deed for them to complete, so that you can praise them for this and help reinforce the benefits of proper behavior.

This method of discipline resembles how a mother disciplines her kittens. Even spraying with water resembles the queen's behavior. A queen will hiss at her kittens to indicate displeasure and the sound of the water spray will reinforce the memory of their mother's behavior. Therefore, they will quickly respond and understand that their behavior is not acceptable.

Dog and Cat Disciplining

To help your dog and cat enjoy learning from you:

- Do not work with your pet when either of you is in a bad mood. Consider using flower or homeopathic remedies. These remedies can help reduce negative emotions—aggression, which clouds judgment, and encourage a more positive learning experience.

- Begin each session with play/exercise, which will allow you and your pet to let off steam. Play/exercise relaxes the muscles and oxygenates the blood to increase mental clarity and stamina.
- Always be consistent with your signals and commands. Follow the same routine as much as possible to reduce confusion and build confidence.
- Make time each day to practice communication. Work together during established training times and during everyday interactions.
- Understand first what you will teach, then teach it. Determine the steps in the process so you do not confuse the pet by giving mixed signals. Be sure the animal is ready to learn the command. For example, do not ask a pet to "stay" before first teaching your pet to "sit."
- Practice one command until your pet learns it perfectly, before you begin teaching another.
- Always end training sessions with a few minutes of exercise/play/fun.
- End the session with your pet eager to continue learning—not confused or frightened.

Without clear communication, your dog or cat will never understand what you want. Determine what words are easy for you to remember and say. Write your own training primer containing the basic commands you will teach your dog or cat, and stick to them. If you say "No!" one day and say "Get out!" the next, you will confuse your pet and he or she will stop responding. Yelling "No!" all the time will cause your pet to become deaf to its meaning. If pets do not respond to your commands when necessary, they could be hurt or even killed. For example, they could run out onto the street or get into other dangerous situations. Your pet cannot understand each new experience and will look to you for guidance. If they do not understand you, they may run off blindly.

Create a training primer, which identifies specific behaviors to be taught and related commands. Most pets should easily understand the following commands.

1. "Walk" quietly on lead with collar and harness. Some people prefer the term "Heel."
2. "Sit" quickly when we stop.
3. "Down" to the ground when instructed.
4. "Stay" in the previously commanded position, and "Come" back to the leader.
5. "Out" (as in, out of there, now!) when noses are in the wrong place, or "Out" (of your pet's mouth), to release objects that are likely to be swallowed.
6. "Okay" to touch, sniff, play, eat, or continue any other activity.
7. "Good (insert term of endearment or pet's name)" to display pleasure with the specific behavior of your pet. I use "Good kitties" when they are collectively being cute and "Good girl" when speaking to a specific female pet.
8. "Car," "Ball," or "Toy," and other names for commonly used objects must be used consistently to build a common vocabulary and minimize stress from poor communication. By naming objects and reinforcing the understanding of these names your pet will feel more secure and sure about their boundaries. It will become clearer to the pet that a "Shoe" is not a chew toy when it is consistently removed with a verbal reprimand and then replaced and reinforced with praise by a "Toy" or other suitable object to chew.
9. "Bed" can be used to mean lie down and be quiet, not time to play! Identifying "Bath" and other necessary routines through naming and positive reinforcement rather than miscommunication and trauma will help your pet.
10. "Piddle" on command is important, especially when you are trying to drive across country, leave the house for the day, or go to bed and have only five minutes to spare.

Simply say the chosen word while the animal is urinating to program the recognition of this term and the associated appropriate behavior. Soon your pet will respond by squatting when you give them the command.

11. "Be quiet" helps to calm a vocal or fidgety pet. Reward the pet each time they respond appropriately. Whenever you need the pet to settle down, they will respond to this command. "Be quiet" works wonders in the veterinary clinic during exams. The proper tone is especially important.

12. "Not now" is a command I give to my pets so that they know for sure that I need some space. I often work from my home office and although I enjoy their visits, there are occasions when I do not have the time to play. They simply nod to me in acceptance of this boundary and try me again in an hour or so. Since we acknowledge each other, they are not frantic for attention and can easily respond appropriately to this command.

I have enjoyed writing training primers for each of my dogs, as it helps me keep track of their expanding vocabulary. Zaezar, my oldest and smartest dog, has a well-established vocabulary of over fifty English and thirty French words. Zaezar and I frequently speak and demonstrate together in public. I soon discovered that in crowds she responded more quickly to the French commands because she could differentiate my commands from the conversation around us. In a competition, the language spoken by the twenty other handlers was not a distraction, and she would never lose her concentration like many dogs in the group.

Zaezar can distinguish between the names of a large number of objects: a car, truck, bus or van; a book, shoe, phone, ball or dish. She understands and quickly responds to simple sentences such as "bring me the small ball." She can pick the correct ball from a group of three different-size balls. She understands, "where is (a person's name)?" and will correctly find and bring or herd a person or pet to me.

When told to "go to the barn" she quickly heads out to the right area. When told to "go get the baby" (her favorite stuffed toy), she quickly responds and can bring the toy back on her own, after having picked out the "baby" from among a dozen other stuffed toys, balls, and bones in her toy box.

Over a year ago, at the age of thirteen, she lost her hearing. By associating hand signals with the words she used to hear, she is quickly rebuilding her vocabulary. Luckily, I had trained her with hand signals as well as verbally for the basic commands such as sit, stay, come, etc., so it was not hard for her to understand me later even if she couldn't hear me.

Some of the hand signals I taught her are based on the American Sign Language. I was most concerned about replacing her two favorite words, "Good girl." I taught her this first so that she could understand when she "got" the other hand signals right. I replaced this phrase with the American Sign Language equivalent for "yes," a closed fist held straight with an up and down motion, to which she now responds with as much enthusiasm and tail wagging as she did when she could hear this praise. Although it is common for a dog with hearing loss to become withdrawn or irritable, Zaezar has suffered no stress thanks to the excellent level of communication and trust we developed over the years. Good training allows you to help your dog through life's challenges without trauma.

ESTABLISHING AND MAINTAINING BOUNDARIES

It is important to establish identifiable, consistent boundaries. Your pet must first understand what is and isn't acceptable behavior before it can be expected to behave. If you do not want your dog to go out in the front yard, do not allow them to go out there one day but not the next. If your cat is supposed to stay off the kitchen counter, do not encourage them to go there or reward them with a nibble of cheese one day and make them get off the counter the next.

Decide what it is that you want but be reasonable. The more reasonable your demand, the more successful you will be in training your dog or cat to identify and understand any boundary. Without this understanding your pet will not be able to follow through with the correct behavior. The trainer, rather than the animal, creates many of the behavioral issues through miscommunication and unreasonable demands.

One of my clients who worked at home wanted her dog to live in the house but was concerned about dirt, shedding, and chewing (that had occurred once while he was a puppy). Her dog was required to spend all his time inside on a small mat in the corner of the living room. The dog was only allowed to leave the mat when he was told to go outside. The dog was locked in a bathroom at night. As a result of her rules, she spent a great deal of time during the day chastising the dog for moving off the mat. Unfortunately, leaving the mat was the only way the dog could get her attention. After a few years of this, the dog became increasingly depressed and developed severe health problems.

During our consultation, I noticed the dog's and owner's neurosis about the mat. After hearing her reasoning about the mat and her concern about the dog's chronic health problems and withdrawal from family interaction, I pointed out the connection between the dog's problems and the stress induced by the mat. We explored how to keep the dog well fed, supplemented, and brushed to cut down on fur and dirt in the house. Since the dog had not chewed anything in years and was now fully mature, I encouraged her to allow the dog to follow her from room to room. She began to communicate to him when she wanted him to be quiet or stay out from underfoot during work times and rewarded him with a playtime at a set time each day and a new freedom to share the home with the family.

After a few weeks of successful interaction between dog and owner, I encouraged her to allow him to roam the house and let him sleep in the bedroom at night, instead of locking him up in their bathroom. The bathroom was to be used only for fifteen-minute time-outs, if needed.

Within three months, my client could not believe that she was living with the same dog. He was enthusiastic about life again, very responsive to her commands, and successfully reversed a chronic disease, previously non-responsive to medications.

My client enjoyed her dog's company and looked forward to doing more things with him. Her unreasonable demand that he stay in one spot, when he craved to be by her side or protecting the house, made him frustrated and depressed and kept her from getting close to her dog. As long as she treated her dog as a possession, rather than a living, feeling being who was sharing her home and life, she had nothing to give him or receive from him.

Consistent praise or disapproval of your pet's behavior is vital to establishing boundaries and to learning the correct commands. Your dog or cat must clearly identify what is or is not acceptable and must make this connection at least fifty to seventy-five times before they will "understand" and not simply react.

You begin to establish general boundaries with your pet by utilizing a time out and rest area for them, providing them with toys and basic communication. Proper training of your pet, and her consequent obedience, is directly related to the clear and consistent boundaries provided by the pack leader (the one who should be reading this book) and the pack (your family, including other pets). Unless you live alone and no one but you will relate to this pet on a daily basis, it is not enough for one person to focus on the training of a pet. It must be a pack effort.

A matriarchal leader raises packs of young pups or kits in the wild, aided by others in the pack who follow her lead and reinforce her rules. The pack leader uses her body language and growls consistently to identify when boundaries have been crossed, uses affection and pride to reinforce positive behavior, and totally ignores the troublemaker when other methods fail.

You, as pack leader, must be willing consistently to put your dog or cat in a time out if needed to reinforce boundaries that are not being respected by your pet. Each behavior must be easily identified and obtainable by your pet and the consequences of inappropriate behaviors must be consistent if they are to be understood by the pet. It is very destructive to both the pet and the rest of the family when one member is attempting to train a pet and another family member is sabotaging these efforts by giving different signals and conflicting behavior reinforcement. Be sure to identify the pack leader, the person who will primarily be in charge of the fundamental behavior guidance and education of this pet. This person will do the basic training, teach commands, and identify the common language everyone will use. The pack leader will also define the methods to correct negative behavior and reinforce positive actions. This will avoid confusion and frustration—the leading causes of behavior problems in pets and their humans.

As pack leader, you will need to intervene on behalf of both animal and human pack members to settle disputes at times, such as who sits on the couch. A pet may automatically come second to a child, but what about another dog? We make equal time for our pets to share prime spots in our home, and, at times, we need to intervene and encourage one pet to give up his or her spot to another that has not had equal time. Our two younger dogs have learned to share without our intervention. They learned from the consistent actions of the pack leader and family members.

Children must understand their boundaries as well, regarding the handling of any animal. Children, not trained pets, trigger most animal bites. If the child shows the pet the proper respect, the pet is less likely to bite or behave badly. Be sure that the children know the proper way to communicate with pets. "No," "Out," and "Bad" should be used consistently and appropriately to describe and reinforce displeasure at something you and your family do not want repeated.

This same concept applies to other animals in the family. If a larger or more dominant pet is picking on another, it is the pack leader's responsibility to reinforce camaraderie through consistent boundaries. Be clear. Be sure a pet has not been reprimanded for behavior triggered by children or other pets.

A pet that reacts out of fear will never be comfortable in training or live stress-free with the family. Trauma does not have to be preceded by severe beatings, abandonment, or torture. Miscommunication and harsh words can break a dog's spirit as easily as physical abuse. Many breeds, especially larger dogs, are often beaten simply because of their size. Yet they have much more tender hearts than smaller breeds. Have you ever seen a five-pound Poodle go after an eighty-pound German Shepherd as if he could win? Smaller dogs may continue to misbehave whether they are physically mistreated or not, whereas, the larger dogs are gentle by nature and will often withdraw from the family or become fear-aggressive.

Although spraying and shrill vocalization can be a common feline reaction to emotional stress, cats do not react as overtly as dogs and usually do not receive the beatings common in dog training. Instead, they appear to suffer more physical illness, which seems associated with unhealthy emotional lifestyles and traumatic miscommunications. Cats' spirits are easily broken and they can be more easily injured physically. They do not have the natural inclination of dogs to be forgiving toward abusers. Simply ignoring one kitten in a litter can produce a withdrawn and timid animal that responds only to her mother and litter mates. It can take years of remedies and trust building to accept human interaction after this kind of abandonment.

Love and consistency in your treatment of an animal is of utmost importance and is the basis of training without trauma. But, love is not enough. I have witnessed many dogs dying at the emergency clinic, recently hit by a car or having ingested a poisonous substance on a walk, who are well-loved but untrained. Only consistent behavioral modification (non-traumatic punishment) and reward for proper actions can properly train a dog or cat, but love provides the patience and nurturing necessary for your pet to develop a good sense of self—which leads to the empowerment a well-trained pet feels.

Science tells us that animals lack cognitive reasoning and "human feelings." I admit that my dogs or cats cannot form a sentence, understand why I choose chocolate ice cream over other flavors, or add numbers in their heads, but they do "feel" emotions such as fear or rejection, and they can learn to communicate with humans. They can "reason" that you go to work at eight o'clock and "anticipate" that you will come home again at a regular time (unless it is your day off, which they will know as well). They can feel your devotion and will respond in kind. It is their nature to be unwavering in their commitment, even if they are beaten or neglected. I believe it is the conflict between an animal's natural instincts and their treatment by us that helps trigger conflict in a pet's mind and creates negative emotions. Dogs and cats want to please us, but if they are never given any guidance or positive reinforcement for good behavior, they can become depressed or ill or they can develop behavioral problems.

BUILDING TRUST

For successful training without trauma, it is of paramount importance that your animals trust you. With trust (a bond), and the approval and rewards they receive from appropriate behavior, your pets will gain a sense of security, and the learning experience will be a positive one. Without trust, the pet will never be completely attentive to you and will become confused more easily when under stress.

Trust is built through consistent handling, providing guidance and reward, and especially through nurturing. Dogs and cats have a strong urge to bond and be as close to their family as possible. In the wild, bonding behavior protects each pack member from the weather and predators. The bonding provides security. Any animal banished from close contact with its pack will quickly die, physically or emotionally.

When cats or dogs attempt to bond, and you misunderstand their signals, punishment can severely undermine their trust. Many owners complain about their getting up on the bed but, to the pet, the bed is the family's nest, the best place to be physically close to you. To be banished is painful. Certainly, I do not like having a cat sleep on my face, but I understand their need to be close to me, so we compromise and share a corner of the bed.

A simple exercise can promote bonding between your animal and you. Sit on the floor next to your pet, gently hold them near, and look into their eyes. Your eyes should convey comfort and love. Often, the pet will wink at you, which is a sign of acceptance and trust. Gently rub the pet's body and talk in soothing tones. Begin with just a few moments the first time, and increase the time to ten minutes each day. As the trust and bond grows, you pet will relax more quickly with each session. Because this exercise will establish trust, in case of an accident or sickness your pet will be able to relax in your arms. This gesture alone can help abate the long-term emotional or physical side effects resulting from trauma.

PROPER HOUSING PROVIDES A SENSE OF SECURITY

Sometimes it is necessary for your pet to live in a protected area. Customize one such area for your dog or cat. This safe place will be useful when you need to get your pet out of the way for any reason: strange men are moving furniture, time-outs are needed, or a destructive pet needs to be secured while you are absent. Having a place of their own will provide them with a stress-free area during potentially stressful times.

Prevention is always the best cure for negative behaviors that result from emotional issues. An animal never forgets its past, including the early years when it was developing a sense of security. A pet will judge all future interactions from the standpoint of past experiences. Security comes from a sense of belonging, which is developed through positive experiences of bonding with the family and the home. These experiences are enhanced by a secure, nurturing place your pet feels connected to. Here they can rest or sleep peacefully; here they are familiar with its accompanying sights and sounds; here they feel safe. If a pet's bed, sleeping area, or kennel is changed frequently, it will always seem strange, it will trigger negative emotional issues, and increase stress.

CRATE TRAINING

Many people recommend crate training, especially for dogs. I believe that people rely too heavily on crating and trigger unwarranted frustration in their adult dogs. Crate training is appropriate for puppies and kittens. In the early weeks of life this crate can be moved from place to place, although it is not advisable to move it around too much. I place the crate by the bed at night, and in the daytime another room or on the porch to provide fresh air and sunshine. The kittens or puppies identify each area and behave differently when placed there. As they grow older, their day area and outdoor parameters are enlarged, but they remain together near the bed at night. Loneliness experienced during bed-time confinement in the kitchen or bathroom can permanently alter the personality of an outgoing puppy or kitten, or a pet of any age, for that matter. This kind of confinement, away from the pack or nest, should only be reserved for time-outs.

Although starting the training of a puppy or kitten in a crate is the easiest way, many animals are adopted when they are older and come from less than desirable beginnings. For these pets, it is important that you establish a safe place/bed for them and a secured time-out area to reinforce behavioral guidance. I prefer using a crate or bathroom to secure my dogs or cats when needed, including for a time-out, and provide them a corner in both the bedroom and living room that is all their own. Beds and toys are kept in both those areas.

Crate training will also come in handy when you travel. It secures a pet in a moving vehicle. It keeps them safe and quiet, away from other pets, while waiting at a vet's. In an unfamiliar hotel room, a crate will quickly settle a pet down.

To train a dog or cat to a crate, begin by leaving the crate open, on the floor, so the pet can sniff around it at their leisure. Do not force them inside, but rather encourage them to explore the crate by placing food and toys inside. After they have gone in and out on their own, encourage them back in and shut the door. Leave the door closed for a few minutes, sit nearby, soothing and praising them. Repeat this the next day for fifteen minutes and again on the following day, this time for a half-hour. Leave the crate open during the day between training sessions so that your pet can explore it. Given the freedom to explore, many pets will seek out the crate as their special place.

The next month (after your pet is very comfortable in his or her crate), put the crate inside the car and induce the pet to go inside. Be sure not to place your pet inside a hot car! If you have an air conditioner, turn it on while your pets are inside, or keep the windows open. As soon as they are comfortable (and calmer) take them for a spin around the block. Teach them to ride in the car before you need to take them to the veterinarian or across the city. This will help prevent travel sickness, vocalizations, and stress when your pet is crated. In addition, your pet will enjoy traveling and look forward to it. Understanding what is happening or what is expected of them will eliminate many behavioral problems.

A crate is a good place to secure your pet during time-outs. Make sure to reward them by letting them out. If the crate is where they must sleep (because you do not trust them) time-outs there during the day are appropriate and may encourage them to change their behavior to gain their freedom at night as well. But if they choose to use the crate as their bed (and you leave the door open), choose a bathroom for the time-out. A bedroom is too comfortable and likely to hold items that can be destroyed by a frustrated pet.

PLAY AND EXERCISE HELP PREVENT BEHAVIORAL PROBLEMS

Now that your pets have safe, peaceful places to rest, it is time to tire them out! Playing with your dog or cat will not only provide great opportunities for you to guide your pet's behavior but also help release pent-up energy.

Playtime is a good time to learn how to read your pet's mood. By engaging in activities that challenge and excite your pet, you will see how they react and learn what signals they use prior to reacting. Each pet has specific signals, but animals use common signals to let us know what they are feeling. This information can be used to gauge how a pet responds to other situations, to their surroundings, or to us, and can help you make choices that will guide your pet's future behavior.

Dogs and cats play different games. Although both enjoy the chase and tumble routine, dogs prefer to wrestle with each other during the day (especially at dawn and dusk), and cats will choose to chase, hide, and pounce at each other, preferably later at night. I recommend you choose to initiate play or exercise at the times that your pet normally would choose it on their own. This way they will be in the play mode rather than the sleep mode, which will reduce frustration.

Interact and play with your pet in a manner appropriate to their needs and temperaments. For example, old or ill pets and young animals cannot play for long periods of time without resting. Pushing your pets beyond their comfort zone, or to the point of fatigue, may trigger negative behavior due to weariness, not due to true emotional issues. However, if these situations are allowed to continue, they may encourage a negative attitude which can later become a behavioral problem.

Dog Play

Dogs love to chase each other, you, or an object. Like the Greyhound that chases a mechanical rabbit endlessly around a track, dogs often prefer the chase to the capture. Dogs will quickly bring back a thrown ball and wait in anticipation of another toss. They love to tug (the backwards chase) and can stay occupied forever on the same end of a ratty rope as long as another dog or person has the opposite end. Part of the chase is to follow the leader of the pack, and dogs love to take walks and hikes with their animal or human pack leaders. You can use their natural instinct to follow and obey their leaders in training them. During playtime and exercise, you and your dog are learning to understand each other. Through this communication, you will teach your dog what their boundaries are and what freedom is.

It is important that your dog has a secure area in which to run freely, at full-out runs when warranted. There is nothing more frustrating to a dog than to stop, turn around, and go (unless it is their idea). They should have a minimum runway of five times the length of their body. A German Shepherd four feet long from nose to tail should have an enclosure no shorter, from one end to the other, than twenty feet. The run can be only four feet wide, but should allow for a good run in one direction.

With the proper size run, your dog can fully extend his body while running, gain structural flexibility, oxygenate the blood, and release energy, just a few of the benefits of this form of exercise. Although jogging or running next to a bike will exercise your pet, "free" runs give your pet emotional freedom and flexibility. Certainly, it is best for your animal to run with you and also exercise freely by himself in a contained area whenever he chooses to.

My childhood German Shepherd, Lady, took herself for a swim in our pool practically every morning around ten o'clock. Although she received little attention from the humans in the household, Lady created a very nice routine for herself. Once she showed interest in the pool, and she had been taught how to use it safely, I created a daily exercise routine, which included a dip in the pool. Since dogs crave routine, she continued this on her own. During the months when my father swam in the pool, she would do laps with him. When I was away at school, she had very little interaction with the family, other than living in the house, being fed, and sleeping in my parents' bedroom. She was not groomed or taken for walks, but she remained surprisingly well adjusted because she had independence and could play when she wanted to. Many behavioral problems arise from boredom, so it is important to allow your dog direct access to a play area to provide daily stimulation.

Within this play area and inside the house as well, provide plenty of toys for your dog to choose from. Dogs will quickly tire of the same bone or ball, unless they become obsessed with it. A dog is more likely to become obsessed with an object if they have no other choices. Although most dogs will eventually show preference for a favorite type of toy, such as a stuffed toy versus a ball or bone, etc., they do enjoy variety. Be sure that the toys you choose are sturdy, without dangerous parts that might be swallowed, and appropriate for your type and size of dog. Vinyl and rubber toys are superior to latex for bigger dogs, while small breeds do best with the supple latex materials. Be sure that the object is large enough for your dog's mouth to prevent your dog from accidentally swallowing the object, which could block the air passage or colon. Be sure to avoid rawhide.

Do-It-Yourself Dog Toys

To make a great tug toy for a rambunctious dog, thread a piece of sturdy wire through a new radiator hose. Make a loop from the hose-wire combination and create a handle from the exposed wire ends. Hang the radiator hose from a tree limb or from a boat spring (for recoil action). You can secure a manufactured tug toy or rubber chew to a line if you do not want to make the radiator hose toy. Natural cotton rope twisted and braided, with a knot or handles at both ends is also great for tugging.

Avoid using socks, shoes, gloves, or any personal items of any type. Your pet won't be able to understand the difference between play items and personal items in the house that they aren't supposed to play with. Examine toys frequently and remove those toys that are battered, especially frayed rope toys, to eliminate choking or intestinal blockage. Supervise all play to avoid accidental swallowing of objects. Swallowed pieces of rawhide can swell up.

Puncture a tennis ball and pass stiff twine through it to tie several together for a wild bounce, or wrap twine around some wood for an interesting fetch toy. Use only non-toxic glue to secure materials together.

Place marbles or small stones and pebbles in a sealed plastic bottle for a rattle that your dog will love to roll. Be sure that the cap is securely fastened with permanent glue. Avoid tossing any heavy toys into the air for a game of catch. Dogs can chip a tooth or damage their jaws if they struggle to catch an object that is too heavy or too hard. Many dogs appreciate an empty plastic soda bottle to make noise with and toss around. Avoid using tin or aluminum cans because they can be punctured by teeth and cut the pet's mouth. A fun dog toy makes a lot of noise, which is why squeaky toys are so popular.

Popular objects to fetch include dense radiator hoses (free of auto fluids), thick wooden sticks, and rolled up newspaper. A newspaper makes a much better fetch-stick than an object with which to inflict fear or pain. Try a twisted and tied length of garden hose to provide a great multi-directional bounce. Frisbees can provide a good game of fetch and exercise at the same time. However, please throw a Frisbee away from, rather than towards the dog. This will prevent him from jumping up and catching it in his mouth, which could injure him. Frisbee-related injuries account for many chronic structural conditions and can lead to paralysis.

Do-It-Yourself Cat Toys

Cats relish quiet toys that they can stalk, swat at, and pounce on. They will enjoy chasing a feather, a ball, or a small container (empty film vials are my favorite), and although some cats enjoy a rattle inside, most prefer the action to noise.

A favorite feline homemade toy is made from a child's fishing pole or wooden dowel, with ten feet of heavy fishing line secured to the end. If a pole is not available then work with the line itself. A small weight is attached, made out of rubber, vinyl, wood, or feathers. Discarded baby toys and teething rings are great. Funky fishing lures are fun once the hook is removed. A thin bungy cord can be substituted for the fishing line if the cat is very rambunctious. This line can be hung from a doorknob, armchair, or under a table so that it can bounce, be swatted at, and tugged.

Cats also love to pounce on objects that will roll around with them. A cloth- or carpet-covered plastic bottle or coffee can will attract a lot of attention. Internal rattles are optional. Many cats enjoy their own babies, and feline-sized fuzzy toys are now available, although you can quickly make one from a human baby's first soft toy or bear. There is always a large selection of inexpensive toys at swap meets and garage sales. Always be sure to remove any objects, such as beaded eyes, which might get chewed off and lodged in a cat's throat.

Nailing a piece of carpet to the wall can make a great scratching post. Better yet, attach the carpet to a corner so that it has two way action for the cat to rub herself. Rubbing is a major form of stress release for cats, and cats who have access to humans, other pets, and objects to rub against and claim as their own, will exhibit less behavioral and stress-related symptoms such as spraying.

Although cats enjoy rope toys, they will quickly chew through and fray the rope, which might be ingested by them. Ingested thread or string can become lodged in the intestines and create a blockage. Ropes can be dangled from secure places, with small rubber rings threaded through and knotted in place. If you provide a variety of accessible toys, your pet will not destroy your furniture, drapes, or personal objects.

Food Toys

One of my animals' favorite homemade toys is anything made from fruits or vegetables! Food can be fun. An apple will be held between the paws and nibbled over for hours, as will a carrot, or celery. Even an olive or a grape can be chased and swatted at. Carrots can be frozen to provide teething relief and entertainment for puppies or kittens. A broccoli stalk with the outer, tough skin peeled can be used whole or sliced into quarter-inch thick circles. These can be rolled, like a coin, across the floor to any pet's delight. Broccoli pieces can also be soaked in tuna juice for exceptional flavor, especially for cats.

Even if you have plenty of toys available, you must still spend time interacting with your pets. This will result in better communication, more play, and stress release for you both.

Incorporating Toys into Games for Training and Exercise

Once you identify the toys your pet enjoys the most, and which ones they will chase or return to you, you can develop games around these toys. For example, if your cat enjoys fetching a small object, spend a few minutes each day throwing this object and encouraging him to fetch it.

This will soon become an easy way to get your cat to run a few laps. This is how we exercise our office cats and encourage them to let off steam when they get too rambunctious during meetings. A few moments will satisfy their need for attention and also tire them out. If we refuse to acknowledge their presence, they simply escalate their vocalizations. When my puppies, now two years old, get too excited, a moment of tugging on a toy with me will focus their excitement. Afterwards, when I ask them to quiet down, they respect my request because I respected their needs. Games can also used during training to help focus the pet's attention or reinforce praise. After a new command is obeyed, do give your pet her favorite toy to play with.

UNDERSTANDING THE PET
WITH SPECIAL NEEDS

You may have to adjust your training practices to accommodate your pets. They may not be mature enough to learn or follow through on certain commands, or they may have suddenly changed their behavior. If we observe our pet's behavior patterns closely, we can often determine what triggered negative behavior and learn how to modify it.

"Baby Time" is often a frustrating stage for caregivers. Puppies or kittens have very basic needs and a limited understanding of the world. Many behavioral issues stem from the caregiver's lack of understanding about how much a puppy or kitten can comprehend and retain. In general, small breed dogs and cats mature at different rates than the larger breed dogs or genetically manipulated feline breeds, such as the California Hairless cat. In your training, consider the pet's level of maturity so you can work more successfully with the babies. To determine your small dog's or cat's level of comprehension, consider each month of life as equivalent to the number one and add up the months of life to compute the competency level for your animal. For example, the command "sit" is the easiest to teach and has a difficulty level of one—a one-month-old pet can be taught this command. Training your dog off lead in traffic has a difficulty level of ten plus, and should not be attempted until the pet is at least ten months old, and has successfully completed basic training.

For the larger dog breeds, who mature more slowly than a smaller animal, add one-half point to every month of age. For example, at six weeks old (one and one-half months), a larger breed dog is ready to understand "sit." You will accomplish this task more easily than if you tried to teach him at four weeks. Larger breed dogs develop physical coordination later than do smaller dogs and cats, who can easily move out of the way or jump up on things earlier than large breed dogs. A larger dog might take a few more months to obtain the same level of coordination. Always work within your pet's comprehension level and within their emotional or physical maturity range.

The Senior Pet may have special needs that must be addressed. After many years of faithful, consistent behavior, an older pet suddenly will refuse to cooperate or begins to exhibit inappropriate behaviors. Frequently, the owner will comment that their pet is acting like a puppy or kitten again. The senior pet might also have physical problems (arthritis, kidney disease, etc.) that are triggering their behavior. They should always be checked by the veterinarian to determine if there is some underlying physical problem. But often changes in behavior are a result of the general decline associated with age. Holistic animal care can reverse such changes in behavior.

The older pet's mental faculties and physical reflexes will slow down. Often, when an older pet stops cooperating, it is due to a loss of hearing or eyesight, a loss of mobility or balance, or can even be the result of a stroke or seizure.

The Stressed or Sick Pet suddenly becomes aggressive or withdrawn, is confused about commands, or simply ignores the owner. That pet is telling you they are not feeling well by not acting well. Behavioral changes are frequently noticed days, sometimes weeks, before the physical symptoms appear or are noticed.

Stress due to pain is the most common physical trigger of aggressive or nervous behavior, while dull aching or fatigue can lead to withdrawal and fearfulness. Loss of hearing or eyesight can also trigger these responses. Cats or dogs who "mark" the house by spraying may be showing the symptoms of a kidney or bladder problem, especially if the behavior suddenly appears and is accompanied by changes in fluid and/or food intake. Eating the walls, shoes, furniture, plants, dirt or any non-food related item may indicate a nutritional imbalance or frustration or jealousy.

Dehydration is another common cause of training problems. The pet that does not receive enough fluids during a day of training can become distracted (spacy) and difficult to communicate with. For example, at a show or competition, a dog can complete the agility course in the morning, but by early afternoon cannot do so. Or, a cat showed beautifully the first day of the show but became more skittish as the weekend progressed. He lost the top award because he refused to let the judge near him for one last look.

Both these animals had faced stressful situations before and always competed calmly and professionally. On the above occasions the pets were dehydrated and, after encouraging oral hydration with electrolytes (at least potassium), both calmed down. It is easy for a pet under physical or emotional stress not to drink enough and, on warmer days particularly, they can become dehydrated quickly.

A pet that is chronically constipated may also display behavioral issues. Constipation creates a back up of toxins in the colon, which are continually re-absorbed into the bloodstream to irritate the nervous system. Pain from impaction or straining to defecate will also weaken a pet and leave them vulnerable emotionally.

If you will consider what events occurred prior to a notable change in behavior, you may discover a physical reason. If you are still puzzled ask a vet to rule out any physical problem, then follow natural care to reverse such changes in behavior.

The Rescued Pet frequently exhibits problems due to past traumatic experiences that the current caregiver may know nothing about. This pet requires more time and energy in order for you to understand the behaviors that you wish to modify. If you are willing to learn and will devote additional attention to observing these pets, rescued animals will always "tell" you what is triggering their moods and behaviors. You may not have witnessed your cat being hit with a rolled up newspaper or a hand. But, if each time you raise a newspaper or hand near your cat, she hides and trembles, it is pretty clear that there is a relationship between your cat's behavior and the action you have taken. Focus on what you observe and you can establish a new understanding and trust.

Behavior Modification

Once you have established yourself as pack leader, defined boundaries, established training methods, and developed a vocabulary, you and your pet can focus on modifying or eliminating specific negative behaviors. Regardless of the type of behavior you wish to change, whether your pet is too submissive, too aggressive, or too hyperactive, these techniques are simple if you and your pet understand the goals.

Identifying the behavior you wish to change and the way to modify this behavior through the verbal and physical (time-out) techniques is fundamental. Behavioral modification should be consistently reinforced daily. The goal should be not only a well-mannered pet when on lead, but also a communicative and responsive pet that is an active member of the family.

Understanding your pet's behavior and taking a more active role in guiding your pet's behavior will help you reach your goal. Interact with your pet as often as possible, even if your interaction is just acknowledging your pet's presence. Mealtime bonding can be especially beneficial. While preparing your pet's meals, talk to your pet in a positive and soothing tone using words that are familiar and pleasing. For example, you can describe what you are doing: "Now I am making such *good* food for you." If you will maintain loving eye contact whenever possible and provide your pet with a peaceful place to eat, you can dramatically change the overall behavior of an unruly pet. Peaceful mealtimes will also help encourage appetite and improve digestion, while reducing finicky behavior. Remember that food itself should also bring pleasure, so be sure that your pet's diet is fresh, tasty, and healthy. Avoid ingredients that may trigger behavioral problems.

Learn and remember your pet's body language and vocalizations. Your pet will show you if they are paying attention or not. They cannot understand what you are attempting to communicate if they are paying attention to everything in their environment except you. Careful attention to your pet's communications will help you understand when behavioral modification is truly needed. When you discipline your pet because you misunderstood their signals, you reduce your pet's trust in your guidance.

During times of stress, my female cat likes to steal my slipper to sleep with. When she was young, she was destructive, so the first time she showed this behavior in adulthood, I feared she would destroy my slippers again. Based on this assumption, I scolded her several times and only created more anxiety for her, increasing her negative behavior. Then I reminded myself to watch her closely to see what she was really trying to do. I saw that if she were allowed to cuddle up with the slipper, she would take a short nap and awaken calmer and more centered. The more I allowed her to cuddle with my slipper, the less she needed it.

Several months later, after I had been away from home for several weeks, she bit into one of my slippers, I removed them from her with a stern look, ignored her, and did not give them back to her for ten minutes. After the slippers were returned to her, she gave me her "grateful" purr and settled right back down with them, never again to bite into one. Since I stopped reacting to her behavior, and instead began to reinforce her positive behavior through consistent daily attention, she stopped trying to get me to react.

GAINING YOUR PET'S ATTENTION AND TRUST

With frequent positive interaction, your pet will pay more

attention to you, understand and perform better for you, and learn more quickly with less frustration. Your pet will begin to trust that you both are communicating the right signals to each other. Gain your pet's attention and maintain it during behavior modification, and you will shorten the training time needed. Earn your pet's trust, and the behavior modification will last a lifetime.

First, in order to gain your pet's attention, you must be aware of the time when she is not paying attention. The best way to gain a pet's attention is to not chase after it. In fact, simply turning your back on a pet will often stimulate her natural curiosity and motivate her to pay attention if only to see what you are doing. It is a mistake to try too hard to get a pet to cooperate. It may reinforce what the pet wants, but in a negative way. If you scold your pet when she is not misbehaving, she will think your reprimands are aggressive and she will have less faith in you.

Your pet will give you many signals that indicate their attention or lack of attention. Recognizing which signals you pet relies on the most will help you.

Nodding and winking usually indicates that your pet acknowledges your presence in a loving and respectful manner. A dog who holds his head up and stares at you directly (in defiance) is not paying attention to your commands and is attempting to dominate you. If, after you have turned the dog in a circle a few times or have given the dog a time out, the dog returns and lowers his head in a nodding gesture and/or gently closes his eyes a few times as if to wink at you, he is acknowledging you as leader and his behavior will improve. Cats, especially, love to wink at their humans when greeting them or acknowledging their command.

Mouthing, swallowing, and/or licking can indicate submission with a willingness to follow and will often accompany

72

nodding and winking. You will see your dog or cat swallow or lick the air shortly after they are given a command, and once more after they have obeyed you. This behavior will frequently occur when a command has been difficult to learn or created anxiety at first. However, if you place too much stress on your pet, they can become overwhelmed with their need to please you, and excessive salivation and foaming at the mouth can occur. If you notice this reaction, rest your pet. Mouthing behavior can be very subtle but once you know what to look for, it clearly indicates when a pet is paying attention. Often pets will lick, or even bite, each other's mouths for comfort, indicating that they are accepted and loved by each other. Some pet owners can misinterpret this behavior as aggressive. Owners may punish pets for this behavior, which can promote poor communication and cause many frustrated owner-pet relationships.

Nosing us indicates that the pet acknowledges us as their main protector, pledges their allegiance to us, and gives us their love. Nosing our fingertips, chins, or mouths, under our arms, behind our knees, or, especially, when they nose our private areas, they are communicating loyalty.

TECHNIQUES TO GAIN YOUR PET'S ATTENTION
Breaking the Spell
When your pet's attention is focused on an action or object rather than on you and your commands, here is an important first step to reclaim their attention. A whistle with a recognizable sound or a loud clap will divert your pet's attention long enough for you to give them a command. If your pet is barking or behaving inappropriately, throw a sealed aluminum can containing pebbles or any other type

of rattle in their direction. Often, this is enough to stop the offensive behavior, reminding them to act differently.

Circle Play

Moving the pet in circles, either by using a lead or by engaging them in play, can also redirect a pet's attention. For example, make your pet follow a feather or a favorite toy or turn them in circle using their lead.

This movement helps to reduce their mental stress and anxiety that may be interfering with learning. This technique is an effective method of reprimand for an unruly pet, since we have learned that *briefly* frustrating the pet (restricting their freedom of movement without trauma or physical pain) can quickly adjust a negative attitude and the *return of that freedom* reinforces appropriate behavior. If this fails after a few tries—the pet continues to repeat the offensive behavior during training time or directly again after being circled—time out is warranted as a means of discipline.

Massage

Massage is a good way to bond with your pet, to relax their muscles (and their tension), and focus their attention on you. A few minutes of massage prior to training can help focus a pet that has become too excited during playtime. A daily ten-minute massage can help minimize aggression in high-strung pets and stimulate withdrawn pets to participate in activities. Gentle touch in a quiet, loving environment can help soothe irritated nerves and fearful perceptions.

USING SUPPLEMENTS TO MODIFY BEHAVIOR

Flower Essences benefit the pet that has trouble paying attention, staying focused, or retaining learned behaviors.

Emotional issues that cause confusion or make it difficult for your pet to understand your intentions can be altered or reversed through the use of flower essences. Your pet's negative behaviors will not change unless emotional changes occur. I prefer homeopathically prepared flower essence remedies (potentized for reliable energetic levels) to the more traditional flower remedies which are made by infusion. Potentized flower remedies have been proven to produce superior results faster than the traditionally prepared ones. Flower essences can be given prior to, during, and following a difficult situation to help minimize negative emotional reactions. They can also be given as frequently as needed to encourage further emotional healing or added to a pet's water for continued support throughout the day. I prefer using the lower potencies (6X to 30C) for general behavioral issues, and the higher potencies (200C, 1M) for deeper, long-term issues or "set" personality traits.

Star of Bethlehem is for learned stresses or accidents. For example, your cat became afraid of the vacuum cleaner because you startled her by turning it on when she was dozing under the bed. Now she doesn't trust the vacuum cleaner and, during house cleaning, she finds a safe place and vocalizes frequently. A dog who is beaten into submission by a trainer and then fears training, or becomes aggressive, is also a good candidate for this remedy.

Willow addresses anger and resentment that prompts aggressive behavior or indignation. These pets suffer from chronic frustration and negative emotions, often becoming aggressive towards themselves, pulling fur out, or obsessively licking to release these emotions and soothe their nerves.

Mimulus is the flower remedy for minimizing fears of all types: fear of riding in the car, fear of going to the veterinarian or groomer, fear of having ears or eyes cleaned, fear of wind, thunder, fireworks, or loud noises, etc. *Mimulus* can help to focus them and to return the level of self-confidence needed to perform well.

Rock Rose is used for present terror. The pet has a specific physical reaction to emotional stress, including excessive salivation, lack of concentration, digestive upset, and shaking. The body or muscles may seem frozen and the pet is fearful to make a wrong move. Unlike *Mimulus*, this remedy addresses both vague and specific fears, as well as the more severe emotional reactions.

Vine is for the overbearing pet that demands attention. This pet engages in negative behavior to get attention. They may be destructive around the house when they don't get enough attention from you. They may vocalize frequently and get underfoot. No amount of attention seems to satiate this animal. Jealousy may be the motive, but it is more likely caused by a lack of proper bonding early in life. *Vine* helps make the pet receptive to the love and attention they receive.

Impatiens quiets the impatient pet whose attention is difficult to gain and maintain. This pet is always anxious to do the next thing, and is usually nervous, regardless of your reassurance, making it difficult for them to focus and learn.

Homeopathic remedies are beneficial to help adjust a pet's emotional filter, so its perception of stimuli promotes the learning process. Homeopathic remedies can be used safely in conjunction with other remedies and nutritional changes. As with flower essences, homeopathy can be used prior to, during, or following stressful situations. Continued treatment can be provided through daily dosages for as long as needed to eliminate or modify their behavior. I prefer using the lower potencies (6X to 30C) for general behavioral issues, and higher potencies (200C, 1M) for deeper, long-term issues or set personality traits.

Aconite addresses behavior caused by sudden shock or fear, such as an accident. *Aconite* helps to minimize physical symptoms, such as stiffness and pain that become worse as a direct result of emotional stress.

Apis is appropriate for the pet that reacts to your sudden movements by nipping at the hands or feet or for the pet that chases after a child or another pet. These pets are often underfoot. They may react to touch as though they have been shocked. This negative reaction to touch may occur from the touch of fabric, a collar, or bath water, or even from temperature changes.

Arsenicum album benefits those pets that suffer restless anxiety, often triggering more aggressive behaviors. This remedy helps calm the pet that paces, vocalizes, or obsessively licks when stressed. It is especially beneficial when illness, allergies, or arthritic symptoms are made worse by emotionally stressful situations.

Gelsemium benefits the pet that suffers from mental apathy and physical weakness due to shock, grief, or stress. Lack of attention results in coordination problems. This pet frequently "bumps" into you or other objects during training or when stressed because they do not seem to be paying attention to where they are walking. This pet wants to be left alone, may tremble, may purse their lips, or may set their mouth when frustrated. They may also suffer from dehydration and/or diarrhea as a result of emotional turmoil.

Ignatia helps reduce grief. Often a pet is grieving the loss of a prior owner or trainer, or possibly the loss of another animal companion. Grief can lead to depression and the pet loses interest in learning and interacting with the family.

This can lead to additional behavior issues or make training difficult. *Ignatia* is a good homeopathic remedy to try when you suspect grief is the cause of the pet's behavior problems. *Ignatia* is a good first choice. It can reduce the pet's depression enough to allow you to address the other underlying behavioral issues with a more specific remedy.

Nux vomica is a homeopathic remedy suitable for the pet who, when stressed, has digestion problems. This pet may be nervous and irritable, overly sensitive to stimuli in general, and disposed to lashing out. Heavy flatulence during training or performance, diarrhea directly following difficult situations, and vomiting can all be related to emotional stress. Constipation is the most likely physical manifestation of chronic stress or frustration in pets who can benefit from *Nux vomica*. This remedy can also reverse a lack of appetite due to anxiety or stress.

Phosphorus reduces separation anxiety and the urge some pets have to follow their owners from room to room or to run away to search for an old family or home.

Herbal supplementation can help either calm or stimulate a pet. Herbs can be used in conjunction with other types of supplementation. They work on a more superficial or physical level than homeopathic and flower remedies; therefore, the two modalities complement each other well. Herbs can physically calm an aggressive pet immediately, while the other types of remedies work on a deeper level to adjust the pet's emotional filter. For example, a pet who is frightened by thunder can be physically calmed with herbs during the first few storms. The herbs help change the pet's perception of thunder. Once they learn that they can feel calm during the thunder and survive it, they will become more confident and this will change their future reactions.

Valerian Root, Hops Flowers, Skullcap, Chamomile, and *St. John's Wort* (which also helps balance hormones), in combination, help relax the aggressive, nervous, or anxious pet, allowing them to rest more comfortably and sleep more deeply. In addition to these herbs, *California Poppy, Catnip, Kava Kava, Lemon Balm, Passion Flower,* and *Wild Oat* also promote general calmness. Herbs such as these support the nervous system physically. When the nervous system is supported, negative emotional reactions during waking hours and especially during training times are reduced. In pets with physical discomfort, which is a leading cause of behavioral problems such as aggression or withdrawal, pain management is improved and muscular tension is reduced.

Yucca, Licorice Root, and *Aloe* can help reduce inflammation of the skin or joints, which may be creating discomfort. Inflammatory conditions are emotionally irritating to the pet and can result in negative or compulsive behaviors.

Siberian Ginseng is an adaptogen and tonic for adrenal stress and helps reduce chronic stress reactions. *Dandelion* and *Peppermint* help improve digestive function during stress.

Chinese Mushrooms, such as *Reishi* and *Shiitake, Garlic, Turkey Rhubarb, Burdock Root, Sheep Sorrel, Echinacea,* and *Golden Seal* are some of the herbs that are useful for stimulating the immune system, detoxifying chemical toxins, and increasing stamina so physical disease is less likely to overwhelm the body. *Bugleweed* and *Motherwort* can help minimize heart palpitations and anxiety caused by stress-induced thyroid imbalance.

Nutritional supplementation is also a vital part of reversing emotional issues resulting in behavioral problems. Nutrition, like herbs, plays a different role from homeopathic or flower essences and should be used with other modalities. The pet that is not well and does not feel well will simply not perform well. It is as important to provide your pet with a healthy, toxin-free diet containing the nutrients necessary for good emotional health as it is to spend time training and guiding their behavior. Poor nutrition will dramatically alter a pet's attitudes and perceptions, reducing their confidence and limiting their abilities.

Be sure to provide your pet with a daily high-quality, high-potency multiple vitamin and mineral supplement. Choose one with higher potencies of *Vitamin B1, B2, B6:* 50 mg. to 100 mg., and *B12:* 50 mcg. to 125 mcg. These levels are appropriate for long-term use in cats and dogs, regardless of their size or weight. For severely nervous, irritated or aggressive pets, double the amounts of these vitamins for the first six weeks of supplementation. Antioxidants, such as *Vitamin A, C,* and *E, Selenium, Zinc,* and *Grape Seed Extract,* are also beneficial in minimizing emotional issues and stimulating health and wellness. The minerals *Calcium, Potassium, Phosphorus,* and *Magnesium* are vital for the maintenance of proper nervous system function, especially information processing and emotional filter development. They also help reduce muscular tension and pain, which can influence the pet's outlook on life.

These general recommendations can help you reverse the majority of behavioral problems. Often, failure in training results from applying set training principles and techniques regardless of how the pet responds. Approaching training from a holistic perspective and supporting the pet's unique needs will lessen the necessity of traumatic training.

These recommendations can be used during any stage of your pet's life, during training, and with any health condition. They are highly effective and will frequently reverse unwanted behaviors. If your pet's reactions are confusing and he is not responding to these techniques, deeper emotional issues may be involved and additional remedies may be warranted. More difficult behavioral situations are addressed in detail in "Addressing Behavioral Dynamics."

Please choose carefully any diets, supplements, or remedies you purchase. Due to the vast differences in products and individual ingredient quality or potency, I have made only general recommendations. Work with your veterinarian and holistic animal care specialist to determine which products and dosage will best suit your individual pet's needs.

Addressing Behavioral Dynamics

Behavioral problems often can be the result of, or associated with, underlying physical symptoms caused by poor diet, chemical exposure, or declining health. Consult your veterinarian to rule out any possible underlying physical conditions that may be creating the symptoms before you address serious or chronic behavioral problems. Trauma or organ failure, cancer, allergies, or arthritis can trigger overt behavioral symptoms such as aggression, although some animals may respond to trauma or disease with nervousness, shyness, or complete withdrawal.

Prevention of a behavioral problem is still the best cure. For example, a pet that is given a calming remedy prior to a new, potentially difficult situation will be less likely to have a negative reaction. The easier a new experience is, the more likely the pet will look forward to repeating it.

Certain emotional dynamics are associated with certain chronic behavioral problems. I have treated many pets successfully with specific flower essence combinations, homeopathic remedies, nutrients, and herbs and have achieved predictable results.

To determine the appropriate remedies for the eight emotional dynamics and the behaviors associated with them, I have evaluated many pets. I first ruled out any veterinary issues, and identified and described the variety of behaviors observed. Each pet was then muscle tested to determine the most beneficial modalities and given an individual remedy or combination until the behavior was modified. Remedies were reevaluated every other week if needed, and changed to address any emotional traits that arose. Other nutritional changes or supplementation are implemented as needed.

During this evaluation period, no physical training was conducted. The pet participated in daily bonding/play exercises, massage, and ten minutes of personal attention. The results of this simple protocol are remarkable.

First, most pets fit into one of eight specific emotional dynamics categories based on their behavioral symptoms. They responded best to multiple remedies in varying potencies (30C to 200C), rather than single remedies.

Secondly, specific behavioral patterns (i.e., spraying or biting) responded to a specific pattern of remedies. For example, flower combinations are excellent remedies to begin a behavioral modification program. Then, if more specific behaviors arise, the use of single flower or homeopathic remedies, nutritional, or herbal supplementation can be alternated with these flower essence combinations.

Observing food and mealtime behaviors is a good way to understand and modify a pet's behavior. In order to teach a dog or cat not to misbehave, steal food, or beg during food preparation and mealtimes, you must understand what motivates your pets to act out.

The pet who displays the "fearful, anxious" emotional dynamic might appear anxious during food preparation. Perhaps these pets remember past experiences in which they were fed a poor diet or had to fight for their share. The aggressive pet may beg or steal food. This behavior may be stimulated by the pet's natural inclination to dominate others during feedings in order to get his share. If you push this pet away or hit it, it will only make them fight harder. The urge to dominate must be modified so that the pet understands that "it is okay to sit quietly and even ignore the food unless you are invited by the pack leader." To reinforce this new behavior, give the pet a treat after mealtime. Once you have identified and understand an emotional dynamic, you can use the appropriate remedies to help modify the behavior. On occasion, a pet will exhibit several dynamics at once. Address the most overt symptoms first and then address other emotional issues as they become evident.

USING DESENSITIZING TECHNIQUES TO MODIFY BEHAVIOR

To desensitize a pet to suspected behavioral triggers (for example, leaving the pet alone results in vocalizations), expose them repeatedly to the trigger for short periods of time (five to fifteen minutes each time), while giving them the appropriate remedies. It can take at least a few days for the pet to understand the new behavior, so desensitization training is a good weekend project. Use the flower combination or appropriate individual remedies before each desensitizing experience and throughout the day. Although this process can require a few days or even a few weeks, you will see a change in your pet's behavior with each positive experience.

In the mealtime example, to modify behavior, expose the pet to their trigger (i.e., food on the table) for no longer than five to fifteen minutes. Praise them when they relax and remove the trigger or remove them from the trigger, and reinforce the correct behavior by giving them your focused positive attention, including a five-minute playtime. This alters your pet's preconceived notions and their reactions to the trigger by altering their emotional filter.

THE EIGHT EMOTIONAL DYNAMICS OF BEHAVIORAL PROBLEMS

Along with descriptions of the eight emotional dynamics, I have included the proper flower combination, additional homeopathic remedies, and behavioral considerations known to work best in these situations. Although each pet is an individual and each situation is unique, your pet is very likely to fit into one or more of these categories. By following the recommendations you will see a decline in negative reactions within a few days. Some pets may need weeks or months of ongoing support for full modification or reversal of certain behaviors, but you should clearly see positive changes to their perceptions, reactions, and behavior during this time. Each episode will be less severe and occur less frequently. If the pet does not become more responsive, you will need to examine other issues that might be implicated or try a different approach to the problem. Although the changes can be subtle or occur more slowly than you desire, you should be able to identify and rely upon those changes, or you are not working with the correct dynamic.

Abandonment Issues

- Flower combination—Use *Agrimony, Gorse, Heather, Honeysuckle,* and *Walnut.*
- Homeopathic remedies—Use *Arsenicum, Aconite, Gelsemium,* and/or *Ignatia.*
- Behavioral Guidance—These pets need reassurance that you will return, they will not be ignored for too long, and/or their environment will remain the same. They respond best to a set routine, such as being fed in the same place at the same time each day until they feel more secure.

The feral cat is an excellent example of the abandoned pet dynamic. They fear confinement yet desperately need shelter and are torn between many feelings. Dogs and cats that become very vocal or destructive when left alone are displaying this dynamic.

This emotional dynamic is associated with homesickness, in which changes in the family or home, isolation for extended periods such as during hospitalization or kenneling, and the loss of routine may trigger depression and anxiety. This pet may try to hide its distress, seem friendly and easy-going, yet pulls at its fur and shows minor obsessive behavior and other stress-related symptoms when left alone. Frustration will also quickly lead the abandoned pet to act out aggressively; therefore, their emotions need to be stabilized. Abandonment is based upon deep-seated feelings that may be the result of an experience that occurred long ago, but is still fresh in the pet's mind and emotional filter. Pets that suffer from chronic abandonment issues often later develop kidney, bladder, and/or digestive ailments.

Aggressive Behavior

- Flower combination—Use *Chicory, Holly, Impatiens, Rock Rose,* and *Vine.*
- Homeopathic remedies—Use *Arsenicum, Apis, Ignatia,* and/or *Phosphorus.*
- Behavioral Guidance—These pets need reassurance that you are in control and/or that their environment will remain the same. They respond best to a set training routine. Additional play/exercise time will help to reduce tension and reinforce good communication skills between you and this pet. Also avoid stress, sudden movements, and abrupt awakening, since these actions tend to trigger an outburst. Many aggressive pets have noticeable improvements in their dispositions shortly after a detoxification process; therefore, proper diet is especially important to prevent a build-up of toxins.

Although aggressive behavior is most often associated with biting, destroying personal property, and malicious vocalization, the overly concerned and possessive pet who demands constant attention in a bullying fashion is also being aggressive. Aggressive pets are often overbearing and difficult to handle. This flower combination helps to minimize general negative feelings that cause a pet to act out quickly, without thinking about the consequences. Anxiety or fear can also trigger aggression. Fear-aggression is a dynamic that commonly results in biting accidents, which usually occur when a nervous pet is cornered. These pets may also be troubled and panic easily. They often suffer from poor digestion, liver problems, or arthritis.

Aggression can become a problem in pets that suffer from chronic, negative, long-term situations or conditions. Often diet and treats, especially those containing sugar and chemical preservatives, contribute to allergic sensitivities and arthritic reactions, which can trigger the aggression. In addition, some animals cannot tolerate the constant irritation caused by painful physical ailments—exhausted from discomfort they lash out when approached.

Fearful, Anxious Pets

- Flower combination—Use *Aspen, Gentian, Larch, Mimulus,* and *Rock Rose.*
- Homeopathic remedies—Use *Arsenicum, Phosphorus, Aconite,* and/or *Ignatia.*
- Behavioral Guidance—These pets need reassurance that you are not threatening them. They prefer calm environments and hide from conflict, literally backing down or away from any perceived threat. They crumble under pressure or discipline; therefore, it is best to focus only on positive reinforcement and easily obtainable goals.

Vague fears and anxieties are common to the pet that responds with apprehension. These pets react with overtly submissive behaviors that can be very frustrating to the owner or trainer. Submission is second only to hyperactivity as a deterrent to learning. Submissive urination is a good example of this emotional dynamic. These pets will shy away from your actions, are troubled, and panic easily. They repeatedly perform poorly because their worry-prone behavior interferes with their ability to pay attention and retain information. They are easily discouraged, lack self-confidence, and are fearful, even of environments and objects with which they are familiar. Fearful and overly anxious pets often are diagnosed with some form of autoimmune or neurological dysfunction, including cancer, allergies, diabetes, arthritis, paralysis, seizures, and general organ failure.

Jealousy and Resentment

- Flower combination—Use *Beech*, *Holly*, *Walnut*, *White Chestnut*, and *Willow*.
- Homeopathic remedies—Use *Arsenicum*, *Apis*, and/or *Ignatia*.
- Behavioral Guidance—These pets need reassurance that they are important and valuable to you, and/or that ongoing changes in their environment will not affect them negatively. For example, when a new baby arrives, introduce the pet to the new arrival as soon as possible and allow the pet to be a part of the daily routines revolving around the baby. Be sure that the pet still receives ten minutes alone with you each day. These pets are happier with a set routine and individualized attention (even if only for feeding, training, or exercise) in the same place and at the same time each day. The more involved they can become in the new situation, the more their jealousy diminishes.

These recommendations work well for general or specific resentments and for jealousy or bitterness. They stabilize the emotions triggered by another person or pet in the household, changes in routine, or changes in the health of family members. These recommendations reduce negative thoughts and anxieties that can also trigger destructive behaviors. Jealousy and resentment can cause health problems that are similar to those caused by fear and anxiety and can also cause an increase in urinary problems such as kidney and bladder stones.

Needy Behavior

- Flower combination—Use *Centaury, Cerato, Elm, Red Chestnut,* and *Vervain.*
- Homeopathic remedies—Use *Arsenicum, Nux Vomica,* and/or *Ignatia.*
- Behavioral Guidance—See recommendations for Jealousy and Resentment.

The needy pet is overly anxious to please the owner while seeking constant reassurance. These pets may also feel inadequate, but are actually so concerned about occurrences in their environment that they don't pay attention, which interferes with their judgment or their retention of learned behaviors. This behavior results in poor performances that reinforces their inadequacies. They can be pushy and are often vocal, needing constant attention, or they may retaliate by withdrawing from you. Needy pets can develop constipation, fur balls, irritable bowel syndrome, urinary, or autoimmune disorders.

Obsessive Behavior

- Flower combination—Use *Cherry Plum, Impatiens, Pine, Scleranthus,* and *Vervain.*
- Homeopathic remedies—Use *Arsenicum, Chamomile,* and/or *Gelsemium.*
- Behavioral Guidance—These pets need to be kept busy with a large variety of activities and toys. They need gentle reassurance and firm boundaries so that they do not become overly obsessive when engaged in activities such as digging or fetching.

"Retriever syndrome," the fixation on an object, often a ball, is the most common type of obsessive behavior. Other examples of obsessive behavior include obsessive licking of their bodies, or another object. They will hold something in their mouths even if food is available, relentlessly guard or bark at "the enemy," or continuously repeat other negative behaviors. They can be quick to act out, yet are also often over-anxious and shy. They never seem satisfied and always need to do better or do more than is required. They are subject to extreme moods and/or mood swings, which are often the result of hormonal imbalances. The flower essences and homeopathic remedies recommended will stabilize the emotions, especially hormonal imbalances that can trigger negative behaviors, including vocalizations and escaping. The obsessive pet may become controlling and pushy. Neurological or digestive dysfunction, arthritis, and allergies can be common ailments found in obsessive pets.

Shock and Grief

- Flower combination—Use *Star of Bethlehem, Rock Rose, Clematis, Impatiens,* and *Cherry Plum.*
  Note: *This remedy should be in every first aid kit. It is excellent for accidents, onset of illness, general stress, and to minimize the effects of any other difficult situation, before or after exposure.*
- Homeopathic remedies—Use *Arsenicum, Gelsemium, Phosphorus,* and/or *Aconite.*
- Behavioral Guidance—These pets need reassurance that they are loved and protected. They are most comfortable in calm surroundings. For a pet suffering from shock or grief, minimize sudden or excessive stimuli. A bed of their own and a comfort toy, pillow, or blanket are very important. At times it may appear that the pet who clings to his comfort object is expressing obsessive behavior, but, as the pet gains in emotional strength, this behavior will diminish.

Grief over the loss of a home, another family member, or a specific daily routine can be difficult for these pets and can result in negative behaviors. Sudden states of panic, terror, or shock can trigger loss of concentration, inability to learn or retain appropriate behaviors, and withdrawal. Many pets react aggressively when stressed, become quick to react, or may be seem desperate. The flower combination suggested, given *before* a difficult event, *during* stressful situations, or *following* a traumatic experience reduces the fear and shock and minimizes the long-term effects that shock might have on the body or emotions. This combination helps return a pet's clarity of mind, gains their attention (especially important if they need emergency medical treatment), minimizes negative reactions by pets overwhelmed by their experiences, and helps reduce the likelihood of a depressive immune response, which is a common consequence of trauma or severe stress.

Spraying and Marking Territory

- Flower combination—Use *Cherry Plum, Elm, Vine, Walnut,* and *Willow.*
- Homeopathic remedies—Use *Arsenicum, Apis, Gelsemium,* and *Nux Vomica.*
- Behavioral Guidance—These pets need reassurance that things will remain the same. They do better with a set routine, such as being fed in the same place at the same time each day. You can try several litter boxes around the house and install doggie doors, but usually flower remedies and set training/play/exercise times works wonders. Be sure to treat any urine spots with enzymes or white vinegar. Do not use ammonia, which has the same basic odor as urine and will continue to attract the pet back to the spot.

Pets who feel driven to continue inappropriate behavior even after punishment are often driven by a strong primal urge to make their point and stand their ground. Feelings of inadequacy or being overwhelmed by a situation, such as changes in litter or box location, foods, household routines, and family dynamics can trigger this urge. Strong-willed pets may seek attention any way they can. These remedies help stabilize negative emotions during transitions, the introduction of new pets, or hormonal reactions. They can help reduce excessive feelings of resentment and bitterness that are acted out more aggressively than seen in the jealousy and resentment dynamic. These strong emotions and reactions can exacerbate medical conditions associated with glands (especially thyroid), digestion, and the eliminatory system.

HOW FLOWER REMEDIES HEAL EMOTIONAL DYNAMICS

Helping the body heal physically and emotionally can often be very frustrating, especially when tools known to work in most cases seem useless. Edward Bach, a physician and botanist, observed that some patients who didn't seem as ill as others did not respond as well to standard treatment. They seemed to lack the will to improve. Dr. Bach identified several emotional and psychological traits which influenced how the patient viewed his illness and identified a variety of plants (flower remedies) that helped patients eliminate their blocks to recovery.

Flower remedies are a gentle, chemical-free method to provide emotional pet care. Unlike humans, animals never doubt the true healing power of a substance simply because they do not understand what it is or how it works. They simply respond to the support they are provided. If one remedy is not successful, at least it will do no harm, and you will know quickly what is or is not working by your pet's behavior.

Owners who choose to use flower remedies to help alleviate a pet's emotional stress, aid in rehabilitation, or prevent behaviors or disease triggered by stressful situations, appreciate the subtlety of these remedies. The result is remarkable, often overnight in fact, although the slow elimination of the behavior over a period of a few days to a few weeks is more usual.

Physical and emotional stress can severely cripple the immune system. It is not uncommon for a pet with a history of emotional stress to develop health problems. When stress is reduced, its body will respond more quickly to the treatments and training will become easier for the pet.

Flower essences can eliminate or change the emotional "filter" through which a pet "perceives" the actions around them. If a pet associates hands with pain from a previous beating (even one that occurred years earlier by another trainer) it will automatically react negatively to your hands on or near its body. When a remedy such as *Star of Bethlehem* is given, this filter begins to change, and the pet will not react as strongly to hands the next time. Each time the remedy (and an associated positive experience) is repeated, the pet will respond positively because the remedy has changed its reaction.

To use flower remedies to reverse specific emotional issues, first identify what personality trait or "filter" you associate more closely with your pet's problems and utilize one or more remedies to reverse this trait. By reversing the emotional trait that may be interfering with your pet's ability to learn and by supporting positive behaviors, your training program will be more successful. Often eliminating the negative trait by adjusting your pet's emotional filter will be enough to make a difference.

THE SEVEN "FILTERS" ASSOCIATED WITH BEHAVIORAL PROBLEMS

The following seven personality traits influence how the pet perceives the stimulus that triggers a specific behavior. If the recommendations for one or more of the behavioral dynamics does not promote the changes you wish to see, further exploration of these traits and the use of additional, individual flower essences may be warranted to alter these filters.

The Strong-Willed Pet—Dominance Filter
Vine

This pet is often overbearing, deliberately using pressure, especially vocalizations and destructive acts, to achieve their goals. This remedy is appropriate for pets who pull at their leads, who repeat negative behaviors even if they have been reprimanded, or who simply ignore your attempts with a clear show of defiance. This is a good remedy for aggressive bullies.

Vervain

Vervain is excellent for pushy or controlling animals who always seem to need attention. These pets are easily incensed and act out whenever attention is paid to another animal or when they feel ignored. They exhibit less aggression than those pets for whom *Vine* is recommended.

Beech

The pets who may need to be treated with *Beech* always seem to seek perfection. They may overreact to small annoyances: to losing their favorite toy to another pet or child, to being put through their training routine for the second time that day (they seem to resent being given the command again), or to having a litter box moved. This is a common remedy for pets, especially bitches who recently whelped, and who resent any intrusion into their domain by outsiders (including you).

Impatiens

Impatiens is useful for pets who are quick in thought and action. They don't tolerate delay of any kind—they are unwilling to wait. This is a remedy for the pet who is over-anxious at mealtime, often to the point of physical reactions such as stomach rumblings, burping bile, or passing gas. *Impatiens*-type pets can be seen as either aggressive or hyperactive; their behavior is triggered by *restraints* whether the restraints are physical (being tied up to wait or asked to "heel") or emotional (being left behind or ignored for a moment).

Negativity (Fear) Filter
Willow

Willow is the remedy of choice when pets have suffered a misfortune and perceived it as unjust or unfair, and displays bitterness and resentment as a result. The most common use for *Willow* is to minimize a pet's need to urinate on your pillow, bed or clothes. *Willow* is a good remedy for any animal who destroys personal property in retaliation. This is a good remedy for pets who have to share their home with an outsider (new pet or human) and becomes destructive or withdrawn as a result, or even attack the outsider or the one they believe is responsible for the intrusion.

Holly

When the pet's jealousy, hate, suspicion, or aggression do not respond to love, *Holly* is a good remedy. This pet, regardless of how much love and attention they receive, cannot live in harmony with the family unit and clearly reacts to these emotions with negative behavior. *Holly* is a good remedy for rescued pets, especially feral cats.

Rock Rose

The *Rock Rose* pet is troubled by states of terror, panic, or hysteria, even if the perceived threat is only a shadow on the wall. These feelings interfere with daily life, make training more difficult, and lead to other behavioral problems such as caving and overt submission, including submissive urination.

Aspen

Pets who benefit from *Aspen* suffer from vague fears and anxieties of no particular origin, and are often apprehensive and full of foreboding. No amount of reassurance, calming herbs, or medication will soothe the *Aspen*-type until they release these vague fears. The *Aspen* pet is more anxious, yet less overtly reactive, than the *Rock Rose* type. This pet is often thin, and may suffer from chronic diarrhea or other digestive problems.

Mimulus

Animals afraid of water, fireworks, thunder, other people, animals, or being left alone respond well to *Mimulus*. Often the animal is timid and shy, and training is difficult. Each time the pet is corrected, the pet exhibits an excessively negative reaction, in particular withdrawal from the family. *Mimulus* is an excellent preventative for timid pets. If it is given before training, it can lessen their anxiety and improve learning.

Crab Apple

Pets who are constantly cleaning themselves, or fear getting dirty or touched, respond well to this remedy. This is especially helpful for pets who have suffered many difficult medical treatments and fear additional handling. *Crab Apple* assists the detoxification processes during illness or general cleansing periods.

Overly Concerned (Nervousness) Filter
Heather
Heather is beneficial for those pets who seek constant companionship and may experience difficulty being alone for any length of time and may become destructive. This is not a true abandonment issue which can be addressed by *Holly*.

Red Chestnut
Red Chestnut is good for those pets who seem overly concerned or anxious for others, always fearing something bad may happen to those they love. They become very reactive when a family member is in pain, is punished, or is mistreated. This remedy is good for pets having difficulty during transitional periods. It should be used with *Walnut* when, as a secondary symptom, the pet is also overly reactive to stimulus. Following the owner around house out of concern or pining by the door until the owner's return is characteristic of the *Red Chestnut* profile.

Centaury
Overanxious to please, often weak-willed and easily dominated by others, the *Centaury* pet reacts more out of fear of their own impending punishment than concern for others. This is an appropriate remedy for pets who fear their trainers, other pets, or family members, yet attempt to please them rather than avoid them. This pet tries too hard, and is so caught up in figuring out what the right thing to do that they often misinterpret signals or commands and end up

making a mistake, which makes them more anxious and prone to repeat this cycle.

White Chestnut

This pet is overly concerned with persistent, unwanted perceptions. They seem to be looking for trouble around every corner and are certain that everyone is trying to steal their freedom. They are difficult to train, since the urge to misbehave is often stronger than the urge to be loved. Often they suffer from sleeplessness as well as irritability. *White Chestnut* will alter the pet's perception and encourage them to focus on the present, not on perceived injustices.

Rock Water

Pets who benefit from *Rock Water* are very strict with themselves. They often rigidly adhere to their habits regardless of the consequences or what they experience around them. For example, if other family pets are playing in the yard, the *Rock Water* pet will remain on the porch because you once scolded him for leaving it. Regardless of your reassurance they refuse to "repeat" their mistake. These pets have difficulty going with the flow, or accepting changes in general, especially the way they are cared for. Move this pet's food dish, or litter box and watch the fur fly. The finicky eater or the hard to please pet will benefit from *Rock Water.*

Chicory

The *Chicory* pet is concerned for others, but needs to control those close to them. Extremely affectionate yet possessive, this pet will often herd other family members, acting as the disciplinarian or den mother. Because they find it difficult to allow those closest to them to have relationships with others, fights occur between pets vying for attention. The

Chicory type pet may seek negative attention by destroying furniture or vocalizing. *Chicory* is good for the bitch who pines after her litter is gone or for the pet who has lost a friend.

Pine

This pet always seems to shoulder great responsibility for the mistakes of others. Even when given away or abandoned, this pet will internalize their perceived failure. They become very upset when others misbehave and will punish the offending party themselves. They will also try to take the punishment of another pet or family member by getting in the way. They act guilty even when they are not. They automatically respond this way to their human's bad mood. These pets want to perform better than they do, never seem to achieve their goals, and do not respond to praise or reassurance as quickly as other pets might. Instead, they will try to perform the command or positive behavior again even though it is not demanded of them. This type may also suffer from anxiety when asked to perform a task they do well, even when they complete the same routines correctly, over and over again.

Indifference Filter
Honeysuckle

Honeysuckle is beneficial for pets who are living in the past, possibly mourning a loss, and are indifferent to their present situation. This is a common remedy for long-suffering pets, either from physical or emotional pain, who seem to have given up on life and refuse to participate. It is especially good for homesickness or emotional withdrawal for newborns or pets who have recently been adopted or have moved to another house. It is also good for pets that react negatively to new arrivals (pets, children, and even company).

Wild Oat

Wild Oat is helpful for pets who suffer from frustration, dissatisfaction, or a lack of fulfillment with their environment or family. Retired show animals or once active animals who are now left behind benefit from this remedy. They are bored with their present situation and exhibit a lack of respect or refuse to pay attention to family members. Once a pet stops paying attention to you, you may become frustrated and ignore the pet, reinforcing the pet's negative feelings. They may suffer from depression and may begin to lack the will to live. *Wild Oat* is often given to pets suffering chronic illness who do not respond to attention and support, or who have lost their appetite.

Clematis

Use *Clematis* for animals who seem to be daydreaming, who lack concentration, and who appear drowsy or spacy. This remedy is for immature pets. Regardless of age, they seem eternally young at heart, in attitudes, or in ability. They seem to mature intellectually and/or emotionally more slowly than others of the same age. They have trouble staying focused on training, and therefore, are slow to retain commands. *Clematis* benefits the pet who recently had surgery or an accident, does not respond well, or is just regaining consciousness. It also helps stimulate any newborn who is not surviving well, by encouraging breathing as well as mental awareness and will to live.

Water Violet

Gentle, independent, aloof, self-reliant, prefers to suffer alone, the *Water Violet* type will try to hide right out in the open. You may feel as if this pet is looking right through you when you are there. This behavior is especially evident in cats. They are not malicious, they simply are ignoring you because, although they might love and trust you, they simply do not need you. They can be handled without overt negative reactions, yet will never approach you or seek comfort from you. This is a good remedy for pets who withdraw from the family with advancing age.

Scleranthus

The *Scleranthus* pets are unable to decide between two things. They suffer from the "retriever" dilemma when deciding between a ball and food. They refuse to release a toy at mealtime and stand there obsessed with the dilemma. They show extreme variations in energy levels or mood and are easily over-stimulated by too many objects, noises, or new commands. A pet who has suffered from neurological trauma, such as a stroke or paralysis, will display this type of behavior, but will gain clarity with this support.

Grief and Gloom Filter
Star of Bethlehem

Star of Bethlehem is beneficial for all types of grief or loss, whether experienced today or years ago. The animals are suffering from the negative effects of a physical and emotional trauma, which results in negative behaviors or actual personality changes. Even years after the trauma, flower remedies can still address the issue that triggers the behavior. *Star of Bethlehem* minimizes the negative effects of separation from loved ones, such as being left in a kennel. This remedy is excellent for other negative experiences due to traumatic training, travel, medical care, accidents, or attacks and can even be used preventatively to prevent emotional issues from developing during these times of stress. It is an excellent first aid remedy or can be used to calm a pet before going to a groomer, veterinary clinic, or entering a competition.

Sweet Chestnut

Use *Sweet Chestnut* when pets have reached the limits of their physical or emotional endurance. They are at wit's end and quickly burn themselves out when stressed. The *Sweet Chestnut* type is often found kenneled in a tiny area and/or lacking adequate exercise (due to owner's inability or the animal's illness or injury). They can also be pets who are naturally high strung. For moments of deep despair and anguish after a long illness, accident, or death in the family, this remedy can stimulate the will to recover and minimize additional emotional strain.

Olive

Olive is good for mental or physical exhaustion when all reserves have been drained, especially after a long illness or traumatic ordeal such as being rescued from an abuser. These animals will often do everything in their power to escape their surroundings, including hurting themselves. They will exhaust themselves trying to get free when kenneled, cared for, or held. The *Olive* pets may become so overwhelmed by their confinement that it creates additional trauma.

Gorse

Use *Gorse* for deep-seated feelings of hopelessness and futility even when there is relief. It is helpful for those rescued pets who do not respond to attention. The *Gorse*-type refuses to eat or to improve, often due to a depressive state, yet with no other overt negative behaviors or symptoms.

Mustard

Use *Mustard* for deep gloom with no known cause that comes on suddenly and lifts just as suddenly, often confusing both the pet and the owner. Melancholia or sadness for no known reason often responses to *Mustard*. Unexplained withdrawal, especially when the pet appears to be healthy, should be addressed first with *Mustard*. Hormonal imbalance, especially adrenal or thyroid issues and allergies, may complicate symptoms. This remedy benefits the bitch in heat and her suitors and encourages a smoother transition into adulthood or during pregnancy.

Oak

Oak personality pets never give up or give in. They struggle on despite despondency from hardships, illness, or overwork. *Oak* is a good remedy at the end of a long illness or recovery from injury. *Oak* supports the pet who does not recognize limitations. *Oak* is good for older animals who will not slow down regardless of their physical limitations.

Overwhelmed Filter
Cerato

Cerato pets are overwhelmed by too many options and too little guidance. Small, yapping dogs or vocalizing cats that become very agitated when more than two people enter a room are *Cerato*-type pets. They cannot decide who needs to be watched or fussed over, and will visit everyone in the room, often getting underfoot. They often react to stimuli by becoming lost in their excitement, clinging to anyone for leadership, yet paying no attention to anyone's commands. The more you try to soothe *Cerato* pets, the more needy they seem to become.

Larch

Even though these pets are very capable, they lack self-confidence or act inferior. This remedy benefits any pets who are always at the bottom of the pecking order. Even if they are the first pet in the household, or are older or larger than other pets, they will give up their position to each new arrival. Anticipating failure, they seem to wait for the shoe to drop, often getting underfoot and unintentionally encouraging conflict. The *Larch* temperament lacks concentration during training or shows, resulting in poor performance. When the remedy is given prior to shows or training sessions, the pet can focus more easily, will pay attention, and feel more confident.

Wild Rose

These pets seem overwhelmed, resigned to their circumstances, and indifferent for no apparent reason. Pets that hide or display aggressive behavior when a new member is introduced into the family respond well to *Wild Rose*. This remedy also benefits grouchy pets who are never pleased and are destructive when their food is changed, during exercise or play times, or when confined to the yard, a room, or a kennel.

Chestnut Bud

Chestnut Bud is helpful for those pets who fail to learn from experience, and repeat the same patterns of mistakes or negative behaviors again and again. These pets feel overwhelmed or defeated. *Chestnut Bud* helps to promote behavioral changes through better awareness and retention of learned behaviors. This remedy changes bad habits, especially when teaching an old dog new tricks. This is also the "let's get along" remedy, helpful for the pet who continually goes against the family rules and remains temperamental, regardless of love, attention, or behavioral guidance.

Cherry Plum

Fearing loss of mental and physical control, the *Cherry Plum*-type seems desperate, almost impulsive as a result of their anxiety. They will bolt at the door, or chase their tails, or chew on objects including their feet, or pull on their fur when exposed to stressful situations, or lash out aggressively when cornered. This remedy is helpful for pets who have lost some mobility or had a stroke and will attack anyone who comes near. They will continue to jump up or move out quickly, even though it causes what they fear most—falling over and losing control. They are very vocal during isolation, heat, or pregnancy, hate to travel, do not tolerate loud noises or sudden movements, and are generally nervous. Strange people or situations can often trigger submissive urination in puppies or dogs and spraying in cats.

"Out of It"(Non-responsive) Filter
Elm

Elm helps pets who display a lack of focus and attention due to feelings of inadequacy, and being overwhelmed by responsibilities (especially during transitions, including birthing and raising a litter, training or competing). They hate experiencing new things and do not respond to new situations. This remedy is very helpful for pets who wander off, bump into things, or get underfoot when stressed. *Elm* is beneficial for pets when they are in social situations such as family gatherings because it minimizes aggressive reactions to stimuli.

Walnut

Walnut assists during difficult transitional periods, such as moving to a new location or new family, or when giving birth, being born, or dying. It helps pets adjust to these new beginnings. This remedy is also helpful for pets who are easily disturbed by changes such as new people in the house, sudden movements, or strange sounds. The *Walnut*-type pet experiences more withdrawal and grief than *Elm* personalities who predominantly act out in response to negative situations and difficult transitions.

Hornbeam

Hornbeam-type pets find it difficult to face situations with emotional content. They seem slightly depressed or tired despite your efforts. This remedy can help the runt of the litter, a pet who is constantly picked on, or a chronically ill pet. *Hornbeam*, in conjunction with *Star of Bethlehem*, is an excellent remedy to help reverse negative associations that may have been caused by long-term physical and emotional abuse.

Agrimony

Agrimony-type pets hide great distress behind a wagging tail. They are willing to participate in and seemingly enjoy daily family events, yet still try to escape physically (bolting) or emotionally (withdrawal from the family). This is a good feral cat or street dog remedy. It reduces the need to escape from their new captivity. This remedy encourages emotional bonding.

Gentian

When pets become discouraged as a result of small delays or hindrances, *Gentian* can quickly stimulate them to relate appropriately. Setbacks during an illness, including the exacerbation of chronic autoimmune symptoms, arthritic and allergic conditions, or emotional setbacks, cause them to give up. This occurs especially during training or when relating to a new family. Unfortunately, the *Gentian* pet can suddenly lose sight of everything positive that has been gained and revert to previously reversed negative behaviors with the slightest provocation.

UNDERSTANDING CURATIVE RESPONSES
When you begin to apply various training techniques, dietary changes, and flower or homeopathic remedies, your pet may respond initially by exhibiting worse behavioral problems than before. There might also be an increase in the frequency of the original behavior for the first few days followed by significant improvement. This is called a curative response and indicates that the body (and mind) is responding.

By watching the way your pet reacts, especially when working with remedies, you will be able to gauge the success of the remedies and when it is time to switch or stop the remedies. Frequently, a response begins within the first twenty-four to forty-eight hours and lasts about the same amount of time. Continue the remedy during this time, but respect your pet's moods—they will soon pass. The behavior may return, especially during stressful times, but will pass in a much shorter period once you give the remedy and your attention to the pet. Each episode of problematic behavior will occur less frequently until the pet becomes more emotionally stable and the behavior is eliminated.

If other behaviors occur, give the appropriate remedies until the behavior is modified. The pet's psyche is built of layers of experiences, perceptions, and reactions. As the most obvious layer is healed the next will show itself. It can take years to fully address the more serious cases, but most pets respond quickly to the more pressing issues first. This promotes the healing of the other, less significant behavioral problems over time and develops your pet's self-confidence, which is the natural consequence to balancing the emotions and strengthening the pet's resolve to behave.

THE CROSSING PRESS POCKET PET SERIES

Allergies
By Lisa Newman
$6.95 • Paper • ISBN 1-58091-002-5

Arthritis
By Lisa Newman
$6.95 • Paper • ISBN 1-58091-003-3

Natural Cat
By Lisa Newman
$6.95 • Paper • ISBN 1-58091-001-7

Natural Dog
By Lisa Newman
$6.95 • Paper • ISBN 1-58091-001-9

Nutrition
By Lisa Newman
$6.95 • Paper • ISBN 1-58091-004-1

Parasites
By Lisa Newman
$6.95 • Paper • ISBN 1-58091-006-8

Skin & Coat Care
By Lisa Newman
$6.95 • Paper • ISBN 1-58091-008-4

OTHER CROSSING PRESS POCKET GUIDES

Pocket Guide to Aromatherapy

By Kathi Keville

In use for more than 600 years, aromatherapy offers a powerful tool for physical and emotional healing. This guide includes a list of the best essential oils for each particular condition, tips on making your own formulas, and special sections on first-aid, childhood problems and emotional well-being.

$6.95 • Paper • ISBN 0-89594-815-X

Pocket Guide to Bach Flower Essences

By Rachelle Hasnas

Bach flower essences provide a remarkable form of energetic healing for yourself, your family and pets. You can learn how to select appropriate flower essences with confidence and use them to bring your body, mind and spirit into harmony.

$6.95 • Paper • ISBN 0-89594-865-6

To receive a current catalog from The Crossing Press
please call toll-free, 800-777-1048.
www.crossingpress.com

7 42851 00695 3

0 0 0 7 6>